THE WORSHIP TARGET

THE WORSHIP TARGET

*Growing Gracious and Holy Affections
through Congregational Worship*

❦

Bradley D. Newbold

FOREWORD BY
Steve Green

WIPF & STOCK · Eugene, Oregon

THE WORSHIP TARGET
Growing Gracious and Holy Affections through Congregational Worship

Copyright © 2024 Bradley D. Newbold. All rights reserved. Except for brief quotations in critical publications or reviews, no part of this book may be reproduced in any manner without prior written permission from the publisher. Write: Permissions, Wipf and Stock Publishers, 199 W. 8th Ave., Suite 3, Eugene, OR 97401.

Wipf & Stock
An Imprint of Wipf and Stock Publishers
199 W. 8th Ave., Suite 3
Eugene, OR 97401

www.wipfandstock.com

PAPERBACK ISBN: 979-8-3852-3159-1
HARDCOVER ISBN: 979-8-3852-3160-7
EBOOK ISBN: 979-8-3852-3161-4

Unless otherwise indicated, all Scripture quotations are from the ESV® Bible (The Holy Bible, English Standard Version®), © 2001 by Crossway, a publishing ministry of Good News Publishers. Used by permission. All rights reserved.

Scripture quotations marked (AMP) are taken from the *Amplified® Bible*, Copyright© 1954, 1958, 1962, 1964, 1965, 1987 by the Lockman Foundation Used by Permission. (www.Lockman.org)

Scripture quotations marked (CSB) are taken from the Christian Standard Bible®, Copyright © 2017 by Holman Bible Publishers. Used by permission. Christian Standard Bible•, and CSB® are federally registered trademarks of Holman Bible Publishers.

Scripture quotations marked (KJV) are taken from the *King James Version*, public domain.

Scripture quotations marked (NIV) are taken from the Holy Bible, New International Version®, NIV®. Copyright © 1973, 1978, 1984, 2011 by Biblica, Inc.™ Used by permission of Zondervan. All rights reserved worldwide.

Scripture quotations marked (RSV) are taken from the *Revised Standard Version*, Grand Rapids: Zondervan, 1971. Used by permission. All rights reserved.

Quotations from Ryan J. Martin are used with permission of T&T Clark. © Martin, Ryan J., 2019, *Understanding Affections in the Theology of Jonathan Edwards: The High Exercises of Divine Love*, T&T Clark, an imprint of Bloomsbury Publishing Plc.

To Janis, who has provided loving support as I wrote this book.
To Seth, Melissa, Sara, Taylor, Cora, Declan, and Josie, who inspire me to make them proud.

To the churches that have given me jobs to support my ministry.

Table of Contents

Foreword by Steve Green | xi
Acknowledgments | xv
Abbreviations | xvii
Introduction | xix

1 The Changing Face of Worship | 1
    Defining Worship | 2
    Targeted Worship | 4
    Worship Wars | 6
    Words Matter | 9
        Passion | 19
        Affection | 11
    Our Journey | 14

2 Old Testament Foundations | 15
    David: A Man after God's Own Heart | 16
    Psalm 22 | 21

3 Jesus: His Role in Congregational Worship | 24
    Jesus: The Object of Our Worship | 24
    Jesus: The Leader of Our Worship | 26
    Jesus: Our Brother, Worshipping Beside Us | 29
    Jesus: Our Place of Worship | 30

4 The Monofilament Line | 32
    New Testament | 33
    The Patristic Fathers | 34
    The Medieval Theologians | 37
    The Reformers | 40
    The Enlightenment | 42

Table of Contents

5 Gracious and Holy Affections (Light and Heat) Part 1 | 46
    The First Sign: Spiritual | 50
    The Second Sign: Transcendence | 51
    The Third Sign: Moral Excellency | 53
    The Fourth Sign: Not Heat without Light | 54
    The Fifth Sign: Spiritual Conviction | 56

6 Gracious and Holy Affections (Light and Heat) Part 2 | 58
    The Sixth Sign: Evangelical Humiliation | 59
    The Seventh Sign: Change of Nature | 60
    The Eighth and Ninth Signs: Christlike Temper | 61
    The Tenth Sign: Symmetry | 63
    The Eleventh Sign: Spiritual Appetite | 64
    The Twelfth Sign: Fruit in Christian Practice | 65
    The Power of Edwards's Work | 67

7 Signs of Nothing 69
    The First Sign of Nothing: Height | 70
    The Second Sign of Nothing: Bodily Effects | 71
    The Third Sign of Nothing: Talking | 71
    The Fourth Sign of Nothing: Outside of Yourself | 72
    The Fifth Sign of Nothing: Recalling Scripture | 73
    The Sixth Sign of Nothing: Showing Love | 73
    The Seventh Sign of Nothing: Multiple Affections | 74
    The Eighth Sign of Nothing: The Order | 75
    The Ninth Sign of Nothing: Over Committed | 76
    The Tenth Sign of Nothing: Praising God | 77
    The Eleventh Sign of Nothing: Boldness | 77
    The Twelfth Sign of Nothing: Confidence | 78
    The Importance of Signs of Nothing | 79

8 The Pattern | 80
    Worship | 81
    False Worship | 81
        Cain and Abel | 82
        The Golden Calf | 82
        Nadab and Abihu | 83
        Saul's Disobedience to the Lord | 84
        Jesus's Confrontation of Tradition | 85
        Ananias and Sapphira's Lying and Stealing | 85

Table of Contents

    True Worship | 87
        Adam and Eve in the Garden | 87
        Worship before the Ark (Davidic Worship) | 88
        The Commissioning of Isaiah | 90
        The Fellowship of Believers in Acts 2 | 91
        A Glimpse of Heaven in Revelation | 92
    Worship and Discipleship | 93

9 Music: Beautiful and Singable | 96
    Musically Beautiful | 97
        Attainability | 98
        Culture | 98
        Preparation | 99
        Quality | 100
    Congregationally Singable | 101
        Key | 101
        Vocal Range | 102
        Rhythm | 103
        Technology | 104

10 Theologically Deep | 107
    Teaching and Admonishing | 108
    Psalms | 109
    Hymns | 110
    Spiritual Songs | 112
    The Right Mix | 114

11 Read, Pray, Worship | 116
    Providing Spiritual Leadership | 117
        God's Word | 117
        Prayer | 118
        Worship | 121
        Guard Your Heart | 121
    Recruiting a Worship Leadership Team | 122
        Lead the Music Well | 122
        Recruit, Recruit, Recruit | 123
        Provide What They Need | 123
        Show Them We Care | 124
    Setting Our Goals for Worship Renewal | 124
    Accepting the Challenge | 126

TABLE OF CONTENTS

12 For the Small Church | 127
    Embrace the Vision | 130
    Find Good Resources | 131
        Find Musicians | 132
        Find Good Songs | 133
        Plan the Service | 136
    Lead Well | 136
    Recommission the Choir | 137
    Conclusion | 138

13 Final Words | 139

Appendix: Resources | 141
Bibliography | 145

Foreword

I'VE ALWAYS THOUGHT THAT my career in the music industry was important, but also non-essential. That's not to say that my writing, recording and concert ministry hasn't been beneficial or useful. I don't have a low view of my life's work; I just have a higher view of the local church. There are only a handful of countries in the world where Christian musicians can have a career in music ministry, supporting a family and those who assist them. On the other hand, in every corner of the globe, regardless of economic, political, or social turmoil, local churches meet regularly to worship the living God. Whether in simple homes or beautiful sanctuaries, God calls his people to gather. In those sacred assemblies, established by Divine authority and Biblical order, He does what cannot be done anywhere else. Our Triune God reorients, forgives, feeds, hears, blesses, and commissions his saints to go back into the places where they live and work. God's called out people gathering to worship is essential.

Throughout the years many have said that my concerts were more like a worship service than a show. I am grateful that in such settings those who attend concerts can be encouraged and strengthened in their faith. I'm thankful for the opportunity to spend an evening rehearsing what is true and providing songs for the faith journey of my sisters and brothers. But the concert is not a worship service. We may sing songs of worship and have some elements of a church service, but we are not a church. We are believers coming together to share music that uplifts. It's an event, not a service.

Worship is much more than many of us imagine. It's not simply the music before the sermon. Its effectiveness cannot be measured by the intensity of an arrangement or the quality of the band. Worship is not a private feeling of passion or an opportunity to demonstrate personal piety. Worship is the entirety of the service that God calls us to so that He can do for us and in us what we cannot do for ourselves. And that happens in the

FOREWORD

context of a local church with its appointed and ordained leaders. As we gather in worship, under the authority of Christ and in reliance on the Holy Spirit, God graciously works in a supernatural way.

I agree with Jamie Smith who stated in his book, *Desiring the Kingdom*, "we are loving beings more than thinking beings." In other words, regardless of what we say we believe, we do what we love. Which leads to the question, how are our hearts shaped to have an ultimate affection for Christ? Our ultimate affection is that which gives our lives meaning, that which determines what we pursue, that which fuels our hopes and dreams, that which defines our ideas about what flourishing looks like. In other words, it's what we love above all else. Our ultimate affection is what we will worship.

Thomas Chalmers once preached a sermon entitled *The Expulsive Power of a New Affection*. But how does this happen?

Our worship services are to be a microcosm of the gospel—a weekly gathering that weaves the gospel into our hearts. Every time we gather as God's people, we are rehearsing the grand narrative of God's redeeming love, acting out through the order of service the Biblical storyline of creation, rebellion, redemption, and the final consummation. In so doing we find our place in His story. Through the physicality of the worship service God slowly transforms our affection for our King and his Kingdom.

A couple of weeks ago I sat in our church service with my three young granddaughters, ages 8, 7 and 5. I prayed that in this rather simple gathering, God would, by the ordinary means of grace and the presence of the Holy Spirit, grow their love for Jesus. Together, we stood and listened to God's call to worship. We sang songs about God's greatness and grace. We corporately confessed our sin and then received the assurance of forgiveness in Christ. At the end of the elder's prayer, we prayed the Lord's Prayer out loud. They drew pictures and colored during the sermon. By memory, they recited the Apostle's Creed, saying words beyond their present understanding, but truths that in time they will come to cherish. We walked together to the front of the church to taste and see the Lord's goodness at His table. An elder called them by name and told them of Jesus' broken body and poured out blood for them. At the conclusion of the service, they reached for my hands and lifted them high as we sang the doxology. Your church service order may look differently, but our purpose and hope should be the same.

Brad Newbold has spent years studying, researching, and now putting into book form an urgently needed resource for all who plan and lead the gatherings of God's people. *The Worship Target* addresses the most vital struggle and need of our lives, a growing affection for Christ. Drawing from Jonathan Edwards' treatise on *Religious Affections*, Brad suggests that if God has intended for the regular times of worship to be a primary means of shaping our ultimate affection, then every aspect of our weekly services must be prayerfully aligned with that purpose. As you read and consider what Brad has written, I pray that God would grant wisdom to discern the kind of worship that He desires, faith to trust God's slow and seemingly imperceptible work in the lives of his people, and joyful endurance to week after week point those you lead to Christ.

Steve Green
Steve Green Ministries

Acknowledgments

WRITING A BOOK IS a story in and of itself. There have been hundreds of conversations that have made this book better; and for those people and those comments, I am deeply grateful. The constant encouragement to keep writing has been instrumental in completing this project. I could never begin to thank all of you by name who have been a piece of the puzzle toward completion, but I am indebted to you for your generous use of your time to listen to me as I discussed the latest chapter or discovery on this journey.

Initially, I want to thank Dr. Sandra Shannon, who edited my papers and dissertation in my doctorate and every word of this book. She has fulfilled the unenviable task of organizing my thoughts when they were the incoherent ramblings of a lifelong worship pastor who loves conversations full of randomness. I couldn't have done this without her kind and gentle help.

One day, in a doctoral seminar, I presented a session from a discipleship course based on this topic; and Dr. Matthew Swain made a statement when I finished. He said, "Brad, you have no idea how God might use this." Dr. Swain, you have no idea how God has used that piece of encouragement along the way to keep me motivated.

My cohort during the DMin included Dr. Josh Erisman, Dr. Rickey Dawson, Dr. Timmy Ray, and Dr. Kevin Uhrich. Those guys have been an enormous help and encouragement both in seminars and since then. Josh and Rickey were particularly helpful as they read chapters of the book and provided terrific feedback. Dr. John Francis, Joe Gregory, Dr. Char M. Newbold, and Dr. Jayna Newbold were others who read the chapters and provided feedback.

In 2018, I flew back from Ukraine beside Dr. Gregory Morrow. Greg has proved to be a significant friend and colleague. He has become a mentor to me in so many ways and provided substantial feedback on the book

ACKNOWLEDGMENTS

and encouragement for the ministry of teaching gracious and holy affections in worship.

Chris Thomson is the discipleship pastor at Concord Baptist Church, and his office is next door to mine. What a strange case of Holy Spirit serendipity in his life to have me next door the entire time I was writing my dissertation and book. Thanks, Chris, for listening and encouraging. In addition, to all the staff and members at Concord who have had to listen to me, I am so grateful for your patience and graciousness in all those conversations.

My ninety-five-year-old mom, Henrietta Newbold, read my dissertation and said, "Brad, if more churches knew about this, it would change their worship for the better." That's not the first time my mom has encouraged and taught me about worship, but I am genuinely grateful for her blessing.

I thank each of my brothers and sisters, cousins, aunts, uncles, and extended family for providing a spiritual foundation in my life. To my in-laws, Jerry and Jackie Ostrom, who have been pacesetters in ministry for over sixty years, I thank you. To my kids and grandkids, Seth, Melissa, Sara, Taylor, Cora, Declan, and Josie (and any future grandkids), you guys are why I could get up every morning and press on in this endeavor.

Finally, Janis. It's hard to imagine you know me so well and still believe in me. You are my rock, and I love you. You always think the best of me. You show me daily what it means to love Christ with true, gracious, and holy affection. You have set the bar high for me and blessed me with abundance.

Abbreviations

AMP	Amplified Bible
CBC	Concord Baptist Church
CSB	Christian Standard Bible
CCLI	Christian Copyright Licensing International
ESV	English Standard Version
KJV	King James Version
NIV	New International Version
RSV	Revised Standard Version
SWBTS	Southwestern Baptist Theological Seminary

Introduction

And you shall love the Lord your God with all your heart and with all your soul and with all your mind and with all your strength. MARK 12:30

MY WIFE, JANIS, AND I lived in Fort Worth, Texas, while I was studying at Southwestern Baptist Theological Seminary. This was a formative time in our lives as we followed what we believed to be God's call. In January 1989, we attended a Steve Green concert in nearby Arlington. Green, who was at the pinnacle of Christian music, walked onto the stage at the beginning of the concert and said, "It is my desire that by the end of this evening, you will have set all of your affections on Jesus Christ." That statement intrigued me.

What does setting one's affections on Christ mean exactly? And how do we, as believers, ensure that that is our objective in worshipping? And how do worship leaders translate that objective into the music portion of congregational worship services?

That night was pivotal for me. I had been sure I was headed toward becoming a lead pastor in a preaching ministry, but God spoke to me in a powerful way during that concert. Since that night, the heartbeat of my life and my ministry has been leading the musical worship in churches and teaching worship ministry.

I have continued to think about the questions that arose from Green's statement since then. I've searched scripture to understand what worshipping Christ with affection looks like. I've delved into the history of Christianity to understand what the affections are, how we know we are worshipping with them, and how congregational worship has changed because of a lack of understanding about what such worship means. Throughout the years, I have heard preachers say that we should be as excited for Jesus as we are for

Introduction

our football or baseball teams. While I couldn't really disagree with those statements, they never felt quite right. I've never felt for Jesus the way I feel when my Missouri Tigers score a touchdown or the St. Louis Cardinals win the World Series. It just feels different.

Then, in 2016, as I sat in a class while pursuing another degree at SWBTS, Dr. Scott Aniol began discussing the distinction between passions and affections and my head metaphorically exploded! What Dr. Aniol explained put Steve Green's statement into the proper context in my mind and led me to more in-depth study aimed at engaging my congregation in life-changing worship. As a church leader, I'm sure that you hope to engage the people you lead in such worship too.

During this time and to this day, congregational worship, especially the music portion, has been an ever-increasing topic of discussion in evangelical churches. Dubbed the "worship wars," these debates over what style of music to embrace in congregational worship have influenced churches of all sizes, locations, and denominations for over forty years. To resolve these issues, church leaders have usually done one of three things: (1) chosen a style and moved forward with it; (2) offered multiple services, each with a different style; or (3) attempted to blend styles into one service. Each has its drawbacks.

Church leaders who choose the first option often struggle with exactly which style to choose and will undoubtedly have a variety of opinions in their congregations regarding which music to use. Some pastors believe that the church will be more effective at reaching certain age groups if the right style is chosen. While this approach might, in the long run, create a feeling of unity in the church, targeting a style of music in the church's worship services may not be the end-all decision that pastors are hoping for.

Option 2 churches seem to be making the best decision to satisfy everyone in the church. They believe that they are being "all things to all people." But does this option create unintended consequences that the pastor may have never considered? What exactly does this choice communicate to church members? Are pastors who choose option 2 communicating to worshippers that the services are about them and not about targeting Christ? Can this approach create a consumeristic church membership that believes the church's worship services are marketed to various demographic groups?

Churches choosing option 3 have been accused of creating worship services that make everyone mad. While the hope is to meet everyone's

INTRODUCTION

needs, these services may, in fact, create difficulties for worship planning and result in a worship ministry that struggles to present all styles well.

Worship leaders are often asked to adopt the specific styles requested by the lead pastor. I remember one pastor telling me that he wanted to see the church move in a more contemporary direction. So, my aim for the years I served that church was more contemporary music. At another church, the pastor said, "I don't care if we sing traditional, and I don't care if we sing contemporary; I want to sing (insert the name of any church) music!" But should musical style be the focus of worship? If not, what should we be targeting in our church's music and worship ministries?

The fundamental issue in the style debate is the target. Should style be our worship goal? My assertion in this book is that the music we choose should reflect what the real purpose of worship should be: growing in our gracious and holy affections for Christ. Focusing on this target through the power of the Holy Spirit in our modern churches will be transformative!

To be honest with you and to provide full disclosure, I have not always thought about worship in these terms. Like many worship leaders, I wanted to see my congregation physically responding to the worship service in ways that let me know I'd reached them. I remember a conversation I once had with a woman who sang in my choir. She came from a more traditional, liturgical background and heard me bemoaning the fact that our congregation was not engaging in worship as I had hoped. "You mean physically responding?" she asked. "Yes!" I responded. She then told me that I can't gauge worship by a physical response. I thought she was from Mars. I thought physical response was *the* gauge of effectiveness in worship. Now, I know she was on to something, and I wish I could ask her again just exactly what she meant.

Worship leaders can observe that the seriousness and participation of those attending services vary widely. Some are bold and passionate, standing and singing powerfully, lifting their hands high, and shouting words of encouragement during the sermon. Others are quiet and reserved, with arms at their sides or folded across their chests. By all appearances, the first group may be worshipping deeply while the second group is just showing up. But appearances are often deceiving. Both groups may be worshipping deeply, and both may just be in attendance. Outward appearances during congregational worship do not give us a very good gauge of how well we are truly leading believers to worship. Our target in leading worship should be deeper than eliciting broad physical responses, and assessing the

Introduction

effectiveness of worship services should involve more than how well worshippers respond physically to the music and the message.

In *The Worship Target,* I examine what worship is, how our congregational focus has shifted since New Testament times, how the words we use to describe worship impact our focus in worship, and how we can mature in worship by targeting a growing affection for Christ. I help you gain a modern perspective on worship based on ancient teachings. Those teachings come from Old and New Testament sources, patristic fathers, medieval theologians, Reformed theologians, and modern sources. One of the major themes in the book is Jonathan Edwards's teaching in *Religious Affections* and its application to modern worship.

Often, our churches are so focused on the pragmatic results of worship that we lose patience when we don't see immediate outcomes. But, in truth, don't we hope our worship services will provide deep spiritual growth for those we lead? The focus of this book is answering this question: How do I target truly gracious and holy affections in the worship times that I lead? In delving into that answer, I will discuss my forty years of wondering and wandering so that you can gain perspective without the travails that I have experienced. I hope you enjoy and are blessed by this journey.

Let's go!

1

The Changing Face of Worship

Yet a time is coming and has now come when the true worshipers will worship the Father in the Spirit and truth, for they are the kind of worshipers the Father seeks. JOHN 4:23 NIV

HAVE WE EVER TRULY reached the time that Jesus was talking about in John 4? Do we worship in the Spirit and Truth? If not, why not? How can our congregational worship times become all that Christ wants them to be? How can we worship in the power of the Holy Spirit and in the Truth of Christ? These questions and many more have plagued me throughout my years of leading churches in congregational worship. Maybe we miss the mark because we're not really sure what worship is or how to know when we are doing it right.

This book will ask you to reconsider some ideas that you have about worship. In fact, as you read, you may have some questions come up that you don't feel are being answered. I'm asking you to press on. I'm asking you to keep reading. This book is fundamentally written in a quasi-chronological fashion. Because of that, some information you desperately need to understand what you are reading comes later. I guess I'm asking you to trust me to answer your questions eventually. I'm praying this process will be a blessing to you.

DEFINING WORSHIP

The word *worship* appears very early in the Old Testament. Undoubtedly, Adam and Eve worshipped God. They were in his presence and surely found great joy in worshipping him. The Bible records Cain and Able's worship in Genesis 4, declaring what they brought to God as their offerings. As Abraham was heading up to sacrifice his son, Isaac, he told his two servants in Genesis 22:5 to "stay here with the donkey; I and the boy will go over there and worship and come again to you." Here, the word for worship, *hawa*, means to bow down, particularly to a deity, and generally refers to worshipping through an act of bowing down. Another common word in the Old Testament for worship was *abad*, which has the fundamental meaning of serving. From these words, we can deduce that worship in the Old Testament combines the acts of bowing and serving. In the New Testament, the word for worship is *proskenuo*, used in Matthew 2:2 to describe the desire of the wise men to find the King of the Jews because they came to worship him. *Proskenuo* also means to bow down and serve.

The focus of Christian worship is not only God the Father but also God the Son, Jesus Christ, performed in the power of the Holy Spirit. But how do we define worship?

Confining the definition of worship to a simple statement presents massive challenges. These challenges include answering, or at least pondering, questions such as these: What kind of worship are we defining? Are we defining worship universally for all peoples of the world? Can our definition be used by Muslims, Buddhists, Taoists, or any other religions worldwide? Can our definition of worship include meaning for secularists or atheists? Are we defining all forms of Christian worship (personal, private, and corporate), or are we only defining congregational Christian worship?

Daniel I. Block recognized the challenges and presented eight brief statements identifying the characteristics of worship to consider in defining worship:[1]

1. "Scripture calls for worship that is true as opposed to false."
2. "True worship involves reverent awe."
3. "True worship is a human response."
4. "True worship involves action."

---

1. Block, *For the Glory of God*, 24–25.

5. "True worship expresses the submission and homage of a person of lower rank before a superior."
6. "While human subordinates may express their humility before human superiors by bowing and prostration, only the divine Sovereign is worthy of actual worship—assuming that we understand worship as veneration of the One who is the source and sustainer of all things and on whom we are absolutely dependent."
7. "True worship involves reactive communication."
8. "For worshippers' acts of homage to be favorably received by God, they must align with his will rather than with the impulses of depraved human imagination."

Bruce Leafblad, retired Southwestern Baptist Theological Seminary professor, defined worship in this way: "Worship is communion with God in which believers, by grace, center their minds' attention and hearts' affection on the Lord, humbly glorifying God in response to his greatness and his word."[2] Participants in a recent discipleship class I taught gave these definitions for worship:

- "Oneness with God"
- "Giving anything your total attention"
- Putting "my thoughts and desires in line with what He says is true"

My definition of worship is this:

> Worship is intentionally setting one's heart and affection on Christ in order to declare His worth.

A logical question then, is "what gives God the most pleasure?" Psalm 149:4 says "For the LORD takes pleasure in his people; he adorns the humble with salvation." Philippians 2:13 says "for it is God who works in you, both to will and to work for his good pleasure." In Psalm 147:11 we find, "But the LORD takes pleasure in those who fear him, in those who hope in his steadfast love." Fundamentally, we give God the most pleasure when we are humble with salvation, work to his good pleasure, and hope in his steadfast love. Worship is overflowing with these realities. The music, prayers, scripture readings, ordinances, and preaching are filled with celebration for salvation, the work of God's people, and the hope that he gives them. This

2. Melson, "Worship: Our Response to His Greatness," para. 1.

definition gives us a much broader meaning for the general understanding of worship, as Block suggests, and will guide our journey together.

Defining worship also involves identifying what we will include in our worship services. Worship leaders have two basic options. The first option (the normative principle) is to include anything in our services that the Bible does not specifically prohibit. Bob Kauflin is an advocate of this principle and states it this way: "We attempt to follow three principles for ordering our services: 1. Do what God clearly commands. 2. Don't do what God clearly forbids. 3. Use scriptural wisdom for everything else."[3] The second option (the regulative principle) is to include only those elements prescribed or modeled in scripture. The regulative principle pushes us into the word to determine what we should include in our evangelical worship services. It also simplifies the worship planning process and frees pastoral leaders from the pressure to throw in the latest and greatest fad in worship. In a Christian worship service, scripture prescribes the following:

- We should read the word. (1 Tim 4:13; Acts 2:42)
- We should preach the word. (2 Tim 4:2; Acts 2:42)
- We should sing the word. (Eph 5:19; Col 3:16; Acts 2:47)
- We should pray the word. (Matt 21:13; Acts 2:42)
- We should see the word by observing the two ordinances of baptism and the Lord's Supper. (Matt 28:19; 1 Cor 11:23–26; Acts 2:46–47)
- We should give. (Mark 12:41–44; Luke 6:38; Deut 16:17; Acts 2:45)

If we want to build our worship on a rock-solid, biblical foundation, we can build it on the resolute declarations that scripture provides us. Following the regulative principle removes the gray areas of a worship service. We know what scripture prescribes, and we follow that prescription.

TARGETED WORSHIP

As our definition of worship reflects, worship involves intentionality. Not only should individuals be intentional in their worship, but worship leaders should be guiding their congregations to worship intentionally. From my experience, I am convinced that to do that we must identify the specific target or goal of worship. We must then endeavor to meet that goal by

---

3. Kauflin, *Worship Matters*, 155.

ensuring that all we do in our worship services (or at least most of what we do) work together to achieve that goal. And that goal, as identified in our definition of worship, is intentionally setting our hearts' affections on Christ, in the power of the Holy Spirit. And it is the Holy Spirit who gives us the strength to succeed. As Edwards states,

> The Scriptures represent the Holy Spirit not only as moving, and occasionally influencing the saints, but as dwelling in them as his temple, his proper abode, and everlasting dwelling place. And he is represented as being there so united to the faculties of the soul, that he becomes there a principle or spring of new nature and life.[4]

Worshipping in Spirit and Truth is the goal.

Although our congregations gather for worship each Sunday, true worship is often the last thing on our minds. Someone once said that you can judge a church's true mission by listening to the conversations in the hallways between services. Are the discussions in our churches about the latest game, politics, or the weather or about what God is doing in our lives? Are we talking about true worship?

Many of us also lose focus during Sunday morning services. We let our minds wander. We center ourselves on Christ and then get lost in distractions, those little things Satan uses to keep us from worshipping. Fixing our eyes on Christ in worship is difficult in the best of situations. Providing a clear target for the worshipper helps us to focus more clearly on Christ. As worshippers, Christians should pursue what Jesus is talking about in John 4:23: "Yet a time is coming and has now come when the true worshipers will worship the Father in the Spirit and truth, for they are the kind of worshipers the Father seeks" (NIV). According to Gerald L. Borchert, "Jesus defined acceptable worship as participating in two revealed aspects of divine reality: 'spirit and truth' (4:23)."[5]

The woman at the well is an exciting study. I've heard preachers say that when Jesus started asking questions about her personal life, she changed the subject. But I believe, instead, that she got to the subject. I think these questions about worship had been in her head for some time, and she finally found someone she thought could answer them. Borchert says,

---

4. Edwards, *Religious Affections*, 73–74.
5. Borchert, *John 1–11*, 208.

> The statements of Jesus in vv. 21–24 are, thus, far more than arguments in a conversation with a woman. They provide a window into the depth of Johannine theology. If the Samaritan woman wanted a theological prophet, she had met one. This prophet did not bite on her bone of ecclesiastical discussion. Instead, he turned her question around so that she was forced again to confront herself. But was she ready for the implications?[6]

Was she ready? Are you? So, the aim of worship, the target, is to intentionally set our hearts and gracious and holy affections on Christ in love, obedience, and adoration to acknowledge and proclaim his holiness and greatness, mercy, and love and to do all of that in Christ, the Spirit and the Truth.

I have read, researched, studied, and prayed over targeting gracious and holy affections for Christ in congregational worship. I am still on a journey to worship Christ truly in the Spirit and Truth, to sort out what is true and what is Spirit-led worship, and to identify and provide congregational worship that will honor God and grow the worshipper.

I've found that focusing on worshipping with gracious and holy affections for Christ is not particularly easy under the best circumstances. It is particularly difficult when we shift the target of congregational worship from true worship to musical style, which has been a major issue in evangelical churches for the past forty years. Whether this shift is made consciously or not, the outcomes are similar: our congregations seek to be entertained rather than to be engaged, to receive what they want rather than to give what the Lord is due.

WORSHIP WARS

Focusing on anything in congregational worship other than gracious and holy affections for Christ leads us away from true worship. The most obvious example of this is the worship wars that evangelical churches have endured for the last forty years. During this time, churches have debated which musical style is best for their congregations. The issue of style, however, has more to do with preferences than with the substance of worship.

We've all encountered the major styles found in modern evangelical churches today: classic/traditional, contemporary, modern, and blended. You may differ in your categorization, but this will give us a starting point.

---

6. Borchert, *John 1–11*, 208–9.

Classic/traditional worship has much variety across the denominational spectrum but usually includes a congregation dedicated to conventional hymn singing, a singular worship leader (possibly with a choir), and traditional instrumentation (piano only, possibly organ, and, in larger churches, orchestra). Contemporary worship is a service that contains a high-energy commitment to current song selections. I'm not sure what the cutoff is in terms of copyright date, but the songs in a contemporary service are new(er). This style of worship follows the mantra that we should start with a "kickin'" arrangement that instantly gets the congregation on its feet. A modern service has a different feel than a contemporary one. It tends to be more subdued in style and may include some songs that allow the congregation to express lament. Modern services still have joyful songs but make room for broader expression. Blended worship combines traditional elements with contemporary or modern elements, be they song selections, instrumentation, or leadership models. In other words, a service that uses entirely traditional hymnody but is led by a worship team and worship band is a blended service. By the same token, a service is blended if it is led by a singular leader, accompanied by piano and/or organ, singing some of the latest copyrights. Feel free to disagree, but I consider services that include elements from various styles to be blended services.

Most churches with one worship service have one style. Churches with multiple campuses may have multiple styles of worship, one for each location. Churches with multiple services often have a different style for each service. This emphasis on style, however, and the offering of multiple options within one church may inadvertently build a sense of consumerism among the congregation. Instead of communicating that the object of our worship is Jesus Christ, we reinforce the idea that worship is about the worshipper.

Style is trendy. Worship is enduring. Worship has to do with adoring, loving, and honoring Christ. When we focus on God and worship him, we find that style doesn't matter. Just as starving people don't quibble about the food set before them, worship that focuses on growing in Christ will meet our needs when we are hungry and thirsting after God. When we focus on style rather than on Christ, we get in the way of true worship. When we target a style instead of Christ, we market our services to meet the desires of the demographic groups that prefer that style. But in doing so, we may also lose our focus on our actual target: Christ.

The Worship Target

During a season when my church was pursuing contemporary worship, I vividly remember one vacation my family took. Although we had to drive back home on a Sunday morning, I didn't want to forego worship with a congregation of believers. So, I told my family that at 10:20 AM, we would take the next exit and stop for worship at the first church we came to. We were somewhere in Indiana, and the first church we saw was Victory Baptist Church. When we walked in, my eleven-year-old daughter said, "This looks like an old-fashioned church." We sat down, I opened the bulletin, and I read at the top, "An Old-Fashioned Bible-Believing Church." I thought, *Wow! They really are old-fashioned and proud of it.* The worship service consisted of hymns and gospel songs, but the congregation sang them with energy and enthusiasm in the strength of the Holy Spirit. Were they genuinely worshipping? I don't know, but I do know that they appeared to believe what they sang. I realized then that style doesn't matter.

I majored in music as an undergraduate and enjoy and appreciate most music genres, some more than others. My heritage, culture, exposure, and personality influence me. I have learned to appreciate genres I don't necessarily relate to on a personal level, and I hope I've learned to see beyond personal preferences when I plan congregational worship services. What matters isn't the style but the message. And, yes, I try to accommodate different tastes in music, but the bottom line is whether any piece of music leads to worship. Are there styles that are more appropriate for worship in church? Of course, there are! Is it my job to tell you which style is best for you? Of course, it's not! Fundamentally, if the style of music is a distraction from who Christ is, then it is the wrong style. I hope that when people walk out of a worship service I have led, they say, "Wow, God is great!" not "Wow, the music was great!"

Unfortunately, worship wars still exist. On one side are those who urge churches to change to more contemporary music to attract younger members, individuals who find traditional church music alien to their lives. They may not have grown up in the church and have no understanding of the tradition behind the music. Outside of church, they listen to music that fits their lifestyles, cultures, and age groups. On the other side are the traditionalists who want the music to reflect what they have always known the church to be. They are often older, although not necessarily, and are usually the most significant contributors to funding the church budget. Losing them because of switching musical styles is a blow to any church. In the middle are those who see the worship benefit of various styles. They may lean more toward one style than another but can enjoy multiple styles and worship in them. Compromise may or may not resolve the issues.

The fundamental consideration behind music choices should be whether they enhance the worship experience or create short-lived physical responses to the music. Does the music help people worship or merely make them feel good because it's what they like? Does the music target gracious and holy affections or passions?

There is no one right music style for worship, but there is one correct answer to the previous questions. If it does not direct us to Christ or lead to true worship, then we need to examine our musical choices more closely. If the music only provides a "feel good" moment, if we are "on a high" when we leave the sanctuary but quickly wilt, if the lyrics we remember aren't theologically sound and biblically grounded, then the music isn't the right music, whether it's traditional, classic, country, southern gospel, rock, or any other genre. We need to rethink our musical selections if they don't promote true worship. If the target of our worship is growing in our gracious and holy affections for Christ, then the music we choose must promote love and affection toward Christ, not just passionate, physical responses to the musical experience. Ending the worship wars, then, also requires us to understand the difference between passion and affection.

WORDS MATTER

Words are powerful. God spoke and brought all creation into being (Gen 1). God speaks to us through his word, and we are repeatedly instructed to study and learn God's word, his law and precepts, to meditate on his word day and night (Josh 1:8; Ps 119:11, 15), to show ourselves approved (2 Tim 2:15). Studying, learning, carrying the word of God in our hearts and minds is one of the highest forms of worship. So, understanding the power of the words we use to describe worship and discuss our relationship with Christ is essential. In that vein, worship leaders need to understand the difference between *affections* and *passions* as those terms apply to true worship.

Language is a living thing, and the meaning and usage of words change over time. Before the Enlightenment (1685–1815), affection and passion and their related words and phrases referred to religious concepts. Their meanings changed significantly, however, during and after the Enlightenment,[7] especially with the rise of modern psychology and the

---

7. Dixon, *From Passions to Emotions*, 5.

coining of terms such as *emotion* to refer to "mental experiences."[8] Since the Enlightenment, the church has comingled these terms, creating great confusion regarding what believers should target in congregational worship.[9] The coinage of new terms and the changes in the definitions and usage of the terms *affection* and *passion* have created difficulties for many people reading the Bible today. And these difficulties, these misunderstandings, affect our understanding of true worship. Taking time to delve into the changes in terminology and their impact on worship will help worship leaders to plan and deliver congregational worship that targets growing in gracious and holy affections for Christ.

Passion

Let's start with the word *passion*. We tend to throw this term around a lot in life, sports, ministry, and worship. The modern definition of passion is "the state or capacity of being acted on by external agents or forces" and "intense, driving, overmastering feeling or conviction."[10] Samuel Johnson, who published his dictionary in 1755, defined the word as "any effect caused by external agency" and "violent commotion of the mind."[11] In writing *Religious Affections* in 1746, Jonathan Edwards distinguished between the ordinary use of affection and passion:

> Affection is a word that, in its ordinary signification, seems to be something more extensive than passion, being used for all vigorous lively actings of the will or inclination, but passion for those that are more sudden and whose effects on the animal spirits are

---

8. According to Dixon, the term *emotion* didn't even exist until the Enlightenment, translated from a French word meaning "a physical disturbance," part of a network of terms including "'psychology,' 'law,' 'observation,' 'evolution,' 'brain,' 'nerves,' 'expression,' 'behaviour,' and 'viscera.'" Dixon, "'Emotion': The History of a Keyword in Crisis," 338.

9. Dixon states, "It is important to add at the outset, however, that prior to the emergence of the category of 'emotions,' the language of 'passions' and 'affections' was used by both religious and non-religious writers on human mental life, and both terms had a variety of different meanings. 'Passions' for example could be used to refer in a vague way to a broad range of impulses and feelings, or to refer to a smaller set of particularly troubling disturbances of the mind, such as anger and sexual desire." Dixon, "'Emotion': The History of a Keyword in Crisis," 338.

10. Merriam-Webster.com Dictionary, "passion."

11. Johnson, *A Dictionary of the English Language*, 526.

more violent, and the mind more overpowered, and less in its own command.[12]

The term wasn't linked to sexual love until the late 1500s, and not until the mid-1600s did we attach the meanings of deep desire or enthusiasm, as in having a passion for playing the piano.[13] All these definitions reflect the impact of external forces on the individual, forces that are not under the control of the individual, forces that act upon us, not that we engender deliberately within us.

In the Bible, Paul cautions us not to let passions rule us, since doing so will lead to one's destruction: "Their end is destruction, their god is their belly, and they glory in their shame, with minds set on earthly things" (Phil 3:19).[14] The Greek word used here for "belly" is *koilia*, which is translated throughout the New Testament in several different but related ways, including "belly," "stomach," "womb," and "birth." Here, Paul uses *koilia* to represent all of the flesh. In Romans 16:18, the ESV translates *koilia* as "appetites": "For such persons do not serve our Lord Christ, but their own appetites, and by smooth talk and flattery they deceive the hearts of the naive." Despite the prevalence of our "good ol' boy" culture that generally applauds us for following our guts, the New Testament perspective of doing so or of following our passions is resoundingly discouraged.

Affection

The meaning of affection has also experienced significant change over the centuries. The modern definition is "a feeling of liking and caring for someone or something; tender attachment."[15] Edwards defined affection as "the more vigorous and sensible exercises of the inclination and will of the soul."[16] Johnson gave as one definition of affection, "state of mind in general."[17] These definitions vary significantly from the definition we accept today. Affection is deliberate and grows over time. We choose to have affection for someone or something. In Colossians 3:2, Paul tells us to "set your

---

12. Edwards, *Religious Affections*, 11.
13. Online Etymology Dictionary, "passion."
14. See also Romans 1:26–27.
15. Merriam-Webster.com Dictionary, "affection."
16. Edwards, *Religious Affections*, 10.
17. Johnson, *A Dictionary of the English Language*, 15.

The Worship Target

affection on things that are above, not on things on the earth" (KJV), which in modern versions is often translated as "set your mind."[18] Paul also urges believers to put on "compassionate hearts" (Col 3:12), which may also be translated "compassionate affection."[19] All three definitions and their biblical directives reflect internalized and intentional states of mind.

By definition, then, affection and passion are opposites, not synonyms. Yet more and more frequently, Christians are called to worship passionately. A favorite analogy some pastors use is to call on their members to get as excited (passionate) about Christ as they do for their favorite sports teams. But worship and cheering for the home team are two different things. The first should be a conscious expression of our love and affection for God Almighty. It is a purposive, voluntary, conscious decision from our hearts and minds. The second is the reaction to what is happening; it is involuntary. We don't think about how we will act or choose when and how to do so; we just react.

We can clearly see passionate responses in our daily lives, especially with sports enthusiasts. I'm a big Mizzou fan and take in the games, especially football, as often as possible. You'll see my devotion to the Tigers if you check my Facebook page. In 2010, Missouri played Oklahoma for homecoming. This was also ESPN College GameDay, the game ESPN chose as the most important one being played that Saturday. The stadium was packed, and nineteen thousand students were gathered on the Quad, an ESPN GameDay record. I sat beside an older gentleman, probably fifteen or twenty years my senior. Oklahoma won the toss and chose to kick; Mizzou received. On the first kickoff, Missouri wide receiver Gahn McGaffie caught the ball and ran the field, eluding several blockers, to score the game's first touchdown. As expected, the stadium exploded; and I fully embraced the man sitting next to me, jumping up and down together like a couple of twelve-year-old girls. Did my mind consciously decide to do this? No. I was passionate, reacting mindlessly to the external stimulus of the Mizzou

---

18. In most modern translations, the translation for the word in this verse is "mind" (which is understandable given the redefinition of the word affection following the Enlightenment). The KJV arguably is the superior translation in using "affection."

19. The Greek words Paul uses for this phrase are *siktirmo splanknon*. *Splanknon*, which is generally translated as "bowels" or "heart," is often translated in the English Standard Version as "affection." The preceding adjective, *siktirmo*, is generally translated as "mercy" but appropriately here as "compassionate." Thus, one may translate Paul's instruction as "put on . . . compassionate affection."

touchdown; and it took a few seconds for my mind to catch up to my body and realize what I was doing.

Some will say I was just emotional, another term that has created confusion about what affections and passions are. As mentioned earlier, the term *emotion* is a relatively new word. You will not find it in the Bible because it did not exist until c. 1570,[20] derived from a French term meaning "a moving, stirring, or agitation."[21] By 1650, the word had evolved to refer to solid feelings; and by 1808, it referred to any feeling. Prior to the Enlightenment, affection was connected with the mind, heart, and intentionality; passion was almost exclusively linked to the flesh, the gut, the belly, and more spontaneous physical responses to whatever was occurring. With the Enlightenment and its focus on the mind and reason, scholars and philosophers introduced the concept of emotions, along with other psychological terms, equating them with affections even though they primarily reflected passions. These changes also led to targeting congregants' emotions, their passions, in worship because such outward manifestations were supposedly reflective of genuine affection for Christ.

However, according to scripture, pursuing the passions and emotions in worship is equal to pursuing the flesh. Scripture mandates that believers put the flesh and its passions to death (Col 3:5). Instead, we are to grow in gracious and holy affections through congregational worship. Doing so is consistent with Paul's instructions to the Christians in Galatia: "But the fruit of the Spirit is love, joy, peace, patience, kindness, goodness, faithfulness, gentleness, self-control; against such things there is no law. And those who belong to Christ Jesus have crucified the flesh with its passions and desires" (Gal 5:22–24).

Understand that passions are not bad in and of themselves; they are a natural part of who we are as human beings. God wires us for both logic and emotion, affection and passion. When we target true affection for Christ in worship, we will find Christ. He will be our focus. As a result, we will also, inadvertently, have a passionate response. When we target passions in worship, however, it will be challenging to grow in our genuine affection for Christ because passions, when targeted, are too overpowering for much else to happen. Steven Stosny says that "emotion is processed 200–5,000

---

20. Dixon states, "'Emotions', unlike 'affections', 'passions', 'desires' and 'lusts' did not appear in any English translations of the Bible." Dixon, *From Passions to Emotions*, 4–5.

21. Online Etymology Dictionary, "emotion."

times faster than thought."[22] If true, I suggest that passions are stirred at the same rate. Therefore, our worship services should be constructed in such a way that a passionate response is not the target. I have found that by targeting a truly deep-level, affectionate worship time, we can both grow in our relationship with Christ and have a joyful (dare I say passionate) experience that honors God in worship.

OUR JOURNEY

Targeting gracious and holy affections for Christ in our congregational worship services takes more than understanding the historical changes in the meanings of passions and affections. We also need to understand the differences in worship before and after the Enlightenment. Understanding how worship has evolved will help us see how to effect the changes we may need in our worship services to refocus on what is truly important: worshipping with and growing in gracious and holy affections toward Christ.

As Christians, we rest on the shoulders of those who have gone before us, so understanding our beginnings in the faith is essential. In the coming chapters, we'll draw a monofilament[23] line from the New Testament writers through the patristic fathers, medieval and Reformed theologians, writers during the Enlightenment and post-Enlightenment periods, and modern writers to show the changing meanings of passion and affection and their impact on worship. We start by traveling back to the days of Moses and David to examine what our spiritual heritage reveals about our worship.

---

22. Stosny, *The Powerful Self*, 71. Quoted in Payne, *Emotional Poverty*, 16. The context for this quote is Payne's educational book discussing de-escalating negative behaviors in the classroom.

23. A singular, nearly invisible line used in fishing. I use this as a metaphor for my search for the word *affection* across centuries of theological writing.

2

Old Testament Foundations

> You shall love the LORD your God with all your heart and with all your soul and with all your might. DEUTERONOMY 6:5

THE BIBLE IS THE rock-solid foundation for worshipping God with gracious and holy affection. Scripture gives us not only God's commands and instructions but also examples for us to follow. From these emerge a picture of what true worship entails and what worshipping Christ with gracious and holy affections looks like in practice. We see how God draws us to him, shows us how to love him, and guides us to worship him more and more deeply.

In the Old Testament, just before the Israelites were to enter the Promised Land, God instructed Moses to speak to his people. He was to remind them again of his laws and precepts and of their need to obey and follow his word. Part of Moses's message recorded in Deuteronomy includes the Shema, considered "the most essential declaration of the Jewish faith":[1] "'Hear, O Israel: The LORD our God, the LORD is one. You shall love the LORD your God with all your heart and with all your soul and with all your might'" (Deut 6:4–5). In the New Testament, Jesus reiterates this command, stating it is not only the first but also the greatest commandment: "You shall love the Lord your God with all your heart and with all your soul and with all your mind" (Matt 22:37).[2] It is fascinating that Jesus adds the phrase "with all your mind" to the Deuteronomic text. Jonathan Edwards picks up

---

1. "The Shema," para. 1.
2. See also Mark 12:30 and Luke 10:27.

on this and makes much of the need to engage the mind in the Christian faith and, for our purposes, to our worship. Historically, the affections are seen to be housed in the upper soul, the mind and heart.

Jonathan Edwards tells us that "the affection of love is . . . the fountain of all affection."[3] The Bible tells us that God is love, that we love only because he first loved us (1 John 4:16, 19). And so, God draws us to him and teaches us through his word and his interactions with us through his son how we are to love (worship) him. Deuteronomy 6:6–7 clarifies this in part: "And these words that I command you today shall be on your heart. You shall teach them diligently to your children, and shall talk of them when you sit in your house, and when you walk by the way, and when you lie down, and when you rise." In other words, in every moment, in every aspect of daily living, God expects us to remember he is God and to love him with our whole being.

From cover to cover, all of scripture is an attempt to call believers to deeply held gracious affections toward Christ. The Bible tells the story of God's love for us from creation to the sacrifice of his son to atone for our sins, from Jesus's resurrection and ascension to act as our High Priest and Mediator before God to Christ's promised return and our transport to heaven. There we will worship God the Father, God the Son, and God the Holy Spirit in perfect alignment with his will. Until then, he has given us his word and the examples therein to teach us to love and to worship him with gracious and holy affections.

DAVID: A MAN AFTER GOD'S OWN HEART

As role models go, David is the epitome of someone who loves God deeply and seeks to grow ever closer to him. King David began his young adult life as a humble shepherd boy caring for his father's sheep. However, Yahweh had grand plans for his life. This grand plan included a request from King Saul to serve as court musician; a triumphant day in front of Israel's army as he defeated Goliath; a deeply devoted relationship with Saul's son Jonathan; a lengthy pursuit and threat by King Saul; many military conquests; installation as king of Judah and, ultimately, as king of Israel. Walter A. Elwell and Barry J. Beitzel sum his accomplishments this way: "David's kingdom

---

3. Edwards, *Religious Affections*, 95.

represented the epitome of Israel's power and influence during the nation's OT history."[4]

Even though both Jewish and Christian parents have held David up as a model to their children,[5] David was far from perfect. His greatest flaws were revealed when he was pursuing his passions. However, what he was at his core was a man after God's own heart.[6] This was his most significant character trait, influencing David's worship and every challenge he faced. In biblical and theological studies, affections and the heart are connected; so being a man after the Lord's own heart equates to being a man who has a heart filled with affection for the Lord. Scripture tells us that God was seeking such a man: "The LORD has sought out a man after his own heart, and the LORD has commanded him to be prince over his people because you have not kept what the LORD commanded you" (1 Sam 13:14). Following the commandment that God set forth in the Shema, David clearly revealed his affection for the Lord in his life and music, standing out as a prime example for believers to emulate.

As a young man, David had a deep faith and dependence on God. When the Philistine Goliath defied God's armies, David told Saul that God would deliver him from Goliath just as God had delivered him from his confrontations with the lion and the bear (1 Sam 17:37). As Elwell and Beitzel state, David "had a reasonable confidence that God, who had helped him encounter a lion and a bear, would aid him against a champion warrior. So, with faith in God and using his ability to sling stones, David killed Goliath."[7]

David's psalms also show that his life and love were consumed in the Lord, not in material possessions: "You have put more joy in my heart than they have when their grain and wine abound" (Ps 4:7). This joy grows in believers as they grow in their affections for the Lord.

Besides being a man after God's own heart, David exhibited several other character traits that add weight to his selection as someone to emulate in worship. He was humble. Born into a lowly position and considered the meekest of his family, this youngest son of Jesse was the last brought forth when Samuel came looking for the next king. David shares his perspective on humility in Psalm 62:9: "Lowborn men are but a breath, the highborn

---

4. Elwell and Beitzel, "David," 581.
5. Kidd, *With One Voice*, 51.
6. See 1 Samuel 13:14; Acts 13:22.
7. Elwell and Beitzel, "David," 581–82.

are but a lie; if weighed on a balance, they are nothing; together they are only a breath" (NIV). Psalm 131 shows his willingness to give God all the praise and glory:

> O LORD, my heart is not lifted up;
>   my eyes are not raised too high;
> I do not occupy myself with things
>   too great and too marvelous for me.
> But I have calmed and quieted my soul,
>   like a weaned child with its mother;
>   like a weaned child is my soul within me.
> O Israel, hope in the LORD
>   From this time forth and forevermore.

Respectfulness was another of David's character traits. Before becoming the king of Israel, David faced challenges from King Saul, who wished to kill him out of jealousy. Despite multiple opportunities to kill Saul, David chose instead to respect him as king and to guard his life. In 1 Samuel 24, David found himself in a position to kill Saul, who entered a cave unaware that David and his men were inside. David refused to take advantage of the situation when Saul fell asleep, even though his men urged him to end things by killing him then and there. Instead, he cut off a small portion of Saul's robe and immediately regretted it. He told his men, "The LORD forbid that I should do this thing to my lord, the LORD's anointed, to put out my hand against him, seeing he is the LORD's anointed" (v. 6). Psalm 31:9 shows the level of stress David was under: "Be gracious to me, O LORD, for I am in distress; my eye is wasted from grief; my soul and my body also." Yet, despite the distress he was under, he showed respect to King Saul as Yahweh's anointed leader of Israel. In doing so, he also showed his respect and love for God.

David was reverent and faithful. He maintained his monotheistic view toward the Lord throughout his life, never once turning aside to idols as other kings did. He declares in Psalm 18:3, "I call upon the LORD, who is worthy to be praised, and I am saved from my enemies." Because of his reverence toward the Lord, David inspires other believers to be reverent as well. And he trusted God. Whenever he encountered a challenge in his life, he turned to the Lord, trusting in him to take care of whatever situation had arisen. Psalm 3 exemplifies that trait:

> O LORD, how many are my foes!
>   Many are rising against me;
> many are saying of my soul,
>   "There is no salvation for him in God." *Selah*
> But you, O LORD, are a shield about me,
>   my glory, and the lifter of my head.
> I cried aloud to the LORD,
>   and he answered me from his holy hill. *Selah*
> I lay down and slept;
>   I woke again, for the LORD sustained me.
> I will not be afraid of many thousands of people
>   who have set themselves against me all around.
> Arise, O LORD!
>   Save me, O my God!
> For you strike all my enemies on the cheek;
>   you break the teeth of the wicked.
> Salvation belongs to the LORD;
>   your blessing be on your people! *Selah*

Trusting God was possible because of God's faithfulness to him. In return, David remained faithful to God.

Kindness and lovingness marked David's life, as shown in his dealings with Mephibosheth, Jonathan's son. David wanted to extend "the kindness of God" to anyone remaining from the lineage of Saul (2 Sam 9:3). He had Mephibosheth, Saul's grandson, brought to him and told him not to be afraid "for I will show you kindness for the sake of your father Jonathan, and I will restore to you all the land of Saul your father, and you shall eat at my table always'" (2 Sam 9:7). David did this not only out of love for Jonathan, his closest friend, but also to honor the "pledge of familial support" he had made with Saul, again showing his faithfulness.[8]

As a leader, David was masterful in his relationships with others. He delegated tasks to those who either had more time to accomplish them or were more qualified or gifted to do so. He recognized others and gave them opportunities to lead his army, guide his construction projects, and, most notably, lead the worship of the God of Israel. Not only did David give

---

8. According to Bergen, "In this chapter David fulfills the pledge of familial support he made to Saul as well as to Jonathan son of Saul (cf. 1 Sam 18:3; 20:42; 23:18; 24:21–22), the one initially positioned in the Saulide dynasty as David's chief challenger for Israel's throne. Through this narrative the biblical writer portrays David as the supreme Israelite example of covenant faithfulness (Hb. ḥesed), the highest virtue in Hebrew society." Bergen, *1, 2 Samuel*, 354.

recognition to those around him, he also gave recognition to the Lord: "I will give thanks to the LORD with my whole heart; I will recount all of your wonderful deeds" (Ps 9:1). Whenever God worked in David's life or his community, David was faithful to recognize what the Lord had done.

Obedience to God characterized most of David's life, with some notable exceptions, including adultery and murder. Both were grievous sins. Yet, in his heart of hearts, he had a deep desire to follow and obey the Lord: "Give me understanding, that I may keep your law and observe it with my whole heart" (Ps 119:34). Because of that desire, each time David sinned, he came to God with a repentant heart, begging God for forgiveness. We see these expressions throughout the psalms, as exemplified in Psalm 25:11: "For your name's sake, O LORD, pardon my guilt, for it is great." Although God restored him from his sins of adultery and murder and did not require his death, David suffered costly consequences for his actions. Four of his sons died: Bathsheba's first son, Amnon, Absalom, and Adonijah. His kingdom faced three plots against the throne: Absalom's, Sheba the Bichrite's, and Adonijah's.[9] His kingdom also faced a plague because of David's sin in conducting a census.[10]

David is an excellent role model because he "is human, fully, four-dimensionally, recognizably human. He grows, he learns, he travails, he triumphs, and he suffers immeasurable tragedy and loss."[11] We can relate to David. He helps us see our need to confess our sins to God with hearts of repentance, to trust in God even in the most catastrophic situations, to love God deeply and affectionately regardless of the situation in reverence and in recognition of his love, his faithfulness, his holiness.

David also showed his love and affection for God through his involvement in designing the temple, establishing the foundation of music, and singing in Judeo-Christian worship. He authored seventy-three psalms, which show clearly that his life and love were consumed in the Lord, not in material possessions: "You make known to me the path of life; in your presence there is fullness of joy; at your right hand are pleasures forevermore" (Ps 16:11). He declared his deep love for the Lord through the psalms: "I love you, O LORD, my strength" (Ps 18:1). His love for the Lord was the most significant factor in his life and propelled him to preeminence. And,

---

9. See 2 Samuel 15:1–18:8, 2 Samuel 20:1–22, and 1 Kings 1:1–53, respectively.
10. See 2 Samuel 24:1–25.
11. Jamieson, *Joshua–Esther*, 6.

in Psalm 132, David vowed to "find a place for the LORD, a dwelling place for the Mighty One of Jacob" (v. 5).

Although God did not allow David to build the temple—that honor was given to Solomon—David faithfully designed its praise: "he writes his songs, plays them for the Lord, offers them in service of God's people, and shapes the corporate singing of God's praise. The Psalms themselves are as much a part of the building of God's house as anything else is."[12] Referred to as "Israel's Architect of Praise,"[13] David appointed Asaph to concretize communal worship, utilized Chenaniah to organize and direct the music in worship, and established instruction in scripture. He introduced the use of instruments in worship.[14] In combination, David set the pattern for worship we have used for the past three thousand years.

PSALM 22

David's psalms are full of expressions of holy affections, and many of the psalms contain foreshadowing of the coming of Christ and his purpose on earth. Chief among them is Psalm 22, often referred to as a centerpiece of Christology. This messianic psalm reveals David's deeply spiritual understanding of what Christ would do for mankind on the cross, powerfully drawing believers toward more profound affection for Christ and a deeper understanding of his supremacy. In essence, Psalm 22 provides the theological undergirding for believers worshipping Christ with holy and gracious affections.

Christians hold deeply the truth that Christ is the only Messiah for all humanity, as Luke reminds us in Acts 4:12: "And there is salvation in no one

---

12. Kidd, *With One Voice*, 68.

13. Kidd, *With One Voice*, 63.

14. Kidd states, "David's commissioning of Asaph is the beginning of a whole new epoch of corporate worship. Beyond this particular occasion, David aggressively works to leave Israel with a tradition of praise, organizing the Levites with Chenaniah as leader of the singers (1 Chron. 15:27) and setting in place commandments for music-making that would be appealed to in future generations (2 Chron. 23:18, 29:25). The Levites in Solomon's day play 'the Lord's musical instruments, which King David had made for praising the Lord and which were used when he gave thanks, saying, "His love endures forever"' (2 Chron. 7:6 NIV). Three hundred years later, Hezekiah is able to station 'the Levites in the temple of the Lord with cymbals, harps and lyres in the way prescribed by David and Gad the king's seer and Nathan the prophet: this was commanded by the LORD through his prophets. So the Levites stood ready with David's instruments, and the priests with their trumpets' (2 Chron. 29:25–26 NIV)." Kidd, *With One Voice*, 67.

else, for there is no other name under heaven given among men by which we must be saved." Because of this belief, christocentric worship is the goal of worship leaders and pastors across the evangelical spectrum. Psalm 22 stands alone in its clarity in showing what Jesus would endure on the cross. Its truthful "here-and-now" meaning also communicates an intense "not yet" message.

Reading Psalm 22 three thousand years after its writing reveals its powerful messianic message. We already know what is to come, what Jesus will endure, and how he will triumph. What many of us may not know, however, is that Jesus is quoting, even singing, this particular psalm in Matthew 27:46 as he hangs on the cross,[15] using both the words from the first verse ("My God, my God, why have you forsaken me?") and in John 19:30b from the last verse ("for he has done it," i.e., "it is finished").[16]

Verses 1–21 are a lament of David's current situation and of his feelings that God has forsaken him. We don't know the exact nature of his problem; but he is clearly in trouble, feeling intense internal pain and separation from God. Verse 2 exemplifies the depths of David's despair: "O my God, I cry by day, but you do not answer, and by night, but I find no rest." With verse 22, however, this psalm takes a dramatic turn, shifting into praise. David vows to praise the Lord when his deliverance comes: "I will tell of your name to my brothers; in the midst of the congregation I will praise you." This turn reflects the same expectation David expresses in Psalm 5:3 that the Lord will hear and deliver: "In the morning, LORD, you hear my voice; in the morning I lay my requests before you and wait expectantly" (NIV).

The joy of King David was his honesty before God. He knew that he could be candid with God, telling of his pain and suffering, of his fears and doubts, and still praise God "in the midst of the congregation" (Ps 22:22). This realization is significant for believers, for the ability to come to God in safety and security regardless of the situation is monumental in growing godly affections toward him. Knowing God's willingness to hear our painful cries allows each of us to develop greater affection for the Lord.

Psalm 22 undergirds an affectionate relationship with Christ. King David points readers to Christ, prophetically sharing the fullness of his sacrifice. Christ knowingly went to the cross with this psalm in mind. The truth and context of Psalm 22 prod us to remember why we love Christ and

---

15. Grudem, *Systematic Theology*, 576.
16. Harman, *Psalms*, 224.

draw our hearts to a deep affection for him. Only through Christ's sacrifice and his generous benevolence may believers embrace Christ with gracious affections.[17]

---

17. Spurgeon eloquently describes Psalm 22 with its christocentric message: "For plaintive expressions uprising from unutterable depths of woe we may say of this Psalm, "there is none like it." It is the photograph of our Lord's saddest hours, the record of his dying words, the lachrymatory of his last tears, the memorial of his expiring joys. David and his afflictions may be here in a very modified sense, but, as the star is concealed by the light of the sun, he who sees Jesus will probably neither see nor care to see David. Before us we have a description both of the darkness and of the glory of the cross, the sufferings of Christ and the glory which shall follow. Oh for grace to draw near and see this great sight! We should read reverently, putting off our shoes from off our feet, as Moses did at the burning bush, for if there be holy ground anywhere in Scripture it is in this Psalm." Spurgeon, *Psalms 1-26*, 324.

3

Jesus: His Role in Congregational Worship

> Now the point in what we are saying is this: we have such a high priest, one who is seated at the right hand of the throne of the Majesty in heaven, a minister in the holy places, in the true tent that the Lord set up, not man. HEBREWS 8:1–2

TO TRULY UNDERSTAND AFFECTION for Jesus, one must know him. Knowing him motivates the believer to develop genuine affection for him. That being so, Jesus is the embodiment of the believer's affection for Christ. In corporate worship, Jesus plays four critical roles. First, he is the object of worship. Second, he is the leader of the church's corporate worship, both our High Priest and our *leitourgos*. Third, he is our brother, worshipping beside us. And, finally, Jesus is the place of our worship.

JESUS: THE OBJECT OF OUR WORSHIP

Most worship leaders have heard pastors say words to this effect: "Just sing about Jesus and we'll be fine." The reason for such statements comes from the biblical understanding that Christ is to be preeminent in Christian worship. Scripture depicts Jesus as co-equal with God the Father and God the Holy Spirit and shows him to be the central object of the church's congregational worship. As Paul declares in Philippians 2:9–11,

> Therefore God has highly exalted him and bestowed on him the name that is above every name, so that at the name of Jesus every knee should bow, in heaven and on earth and under the earth, and

Jesus: His Role in Congregational Worship

every tongue confess that Jesus Christ is Lord, to the glory of God the Father.

Jesus Christ is truly God and truly man. He lived a sinless life and ministered with grace: "And being found in human form, he humbled himself by becoming obedient to the point of death, even death on a cross" (Phil 2:8). Therefore, he is deserving of unfettered, purely focused worship.

The hymn Paul quotes in Philippians 2 parallels the worship Jesus received from the wise men at his birth: "And going into the house, they saw the child with Mary his mother, and they fell down and worshiped him" (Matt 2:11a). Bowing in worship before Christ is either a current reality for every individual, with all the joys and blessings of following Christ, or a later reality that will be devoid of the hopes and joys associated with faith in Christ, as John Risbridger reminds us: "all is fulfilled by Christ; therefore, all will worship Christ."[1]

Logically and biblically, if we are followers of Christ, we are also Christ worshippers and worship him exclusively. As the object of worship, he inspires us to grow in gracious affection toward him. Yet, because of sin, many people choose not to worship him or do not worship him fully, even if they know him. Sin can often derail even the sincerest adherents from devotion to Christ and the centrality of Christ in worship. Paradoxically, the music designed to worship Christ can distract us from the true object of worship. Music can be a distraction from worship anytime it is the overwhelming aspect of our services. If the congregation walks out talking more about music than the God of the music, then we have missed our target.

Unexpectedly, most worship pastors do not love hearing comments like these: "Wow, the music was great today!" Of course, these comments are better than hearing that the music was bad or out of tune. But, in reality, most worship pastors prefer to hear comments about the powerful texts of the songs or meaningfulness of the scripture readings in the service. I was blessed recently when a deacon in our church told me that the songs that I choose truly follow the scriptures. That is the hope, of course, but to hear it from a longtime member of the church is deeply encouraging. Every well-intentioned worship pastor hopes that the texts of the songs he chooses are biblical and that the music does not overpower the text.

As Christians, we all have deep spiritual needs. Perhaps the most pressing of those needs is to worship Christ in the power of the Holy Spirit. If we were to create a spiritual hierarchy of needs, worship would

---

1. Risbridger, *The Message of Worship*, 135.

be at the top. While worship is discipleship, worship is also the purpose of discipleship. Evangelism, fellowship, discipleship, and all other Christian disciplines ultimately create worshippers. Keeping Christ as the object of believers' worship is essential to growing gracious affection for him.

JESUS: THE LEADER OF OUR WORSHIP

Identifying the true worship leader in any Christian worship service is the key to fully understanding and embracing worship. Historically, the person leading the music in evangelical churches is the worship leader, reflected in the many different names used to designate him as such: song leader, music leader, choir director, minister of music, worship leader, worship pastor, and lead worshipper, among others. Each of these titles has merit. Our worship services at CBC start with our deacon of the week reading scripture and praying. He is a worship leader. Then, the music team begins to lead the music. All of them are worship leaders. After the music, my pastor preaches a message from the word of God. He is also a worship leader. However, none of these can claim to be the true worship leader.

The author of the book of Hebrews gives insight into who leads us in worship: "Now the point in what we are saying is this: we have such a high priest, one who is seated at the right hand of the throne of the Majesty in heaven, a minister in the holy places, in the true tent that the Lord set up, not man" (Heb 8:1–2). This text contains two significant, parallel points: Jesus both (1) sits at the right hand of the Father and (2) is our *leitourgos* (minister). These concepts are profound, providing a proper understanding of Jesus as the liturgical leader.

Jesus Christ is our High Priest, but what does that mean? The book of Hebrews identifies Jesus's role as High Priest involves the following:

- He is one who makes propitiation for our sins (2:17).
- He is the High Priest of our confession (3:1).
- He is one who has passed through the heavens (4:14).
- He sympathizes with our weaknesses having been tempted just as we are (4:15).
- He acts on behalf of men (5:1).
- He was appointed by his father (5:5).
- He is High Priest forever in the order of Melchizedek (5:10; 6:20).

- He was unstained (7:26).
- He was one who offers himself up as the sacrifice (7:27).
- He has been made perfect forever (7:28).
- He is seated at the right hand of God the Father (8:1).
- He had something to offer, which was much more excellent than previous high priests had been appointed to do (8:3).

As High Priest, the incarnate God, Jesus is our intercessor. He is our mediator. He was the only High Priest that could fulfill the demands of the law. Hebrews 7:23–25 states,

> The former priests were many in number, because they were prevented by death from continuing in office, but he holds his priesthood permanently, because he continues forever. Consequently, he is able to save to the uttermost those who draw near to God through him, since he always lives to make intercession for them.

Jesus will never be prevented from being our High Priest. He has made a way for us to enjoy him forever, celebrating in his presence alongside the throngs that have bowed a knee to him in worshipful surrender.

Being seated at the right hand of God is also significant because no high priest from the order of Levi ever sat while carrying out his duties. As David Allen notes in his commentary, "there was no chair in the holy of holies."[2] Every other high priest was required to continually offer sacrifices for the sin of the people. Being seated indicates Jesus had completed the work he was sent to accomplish. No other high priest could ever make such a claim, as we see clearly in Hebrews 10:11–14:

> And every priest stands daily at his service, offering repeatedly the same sacrifices, which can never take away sins. But when Christ had offered for all time a single sacrifice for sins, he sat down at the right hand of God, waiting from that time until his enemies should be made a footstool for his feet. For by a single offering he has perfected for all time those who are being sanctified.

Christ's being and his work are why we worship him!

As our worship leader, Jesus is also our *leitourgos* (Heb 8:2). The definition of this Greek word is "a public servant, i.e., a functionary in the Temple

---

2. Allen, *Hebrews*, 440.

The Worship Target

or Gospel, or a worshipper (of God) or benefactor (of man): - minister."[3] The English Standard Version translates this word as "minister" in the holy places.[4] As our *leitourgos*, Jesus leads believers in worship. The church's job is to follow him.[5]

I was surprised recently when I heard Alistair Begg preach on this very topic. His message was entitled "Pastor, You Are Not the Worship Leader."[6] I felt like he was preaching my book. He quoted Hebrews chapters 2 and 8 and Psalm 22. His initial assignment was to say that the pastor of the church *is* the worship leader. But instead, he said, "Neither myself nor the music person is the worship leader." He said that Jesus is present in the congregation and, if he is present, then he does four things:

1. He makes worship possible for us.
2. He gives access to the Father through the Holy Spirit.
3. Jesus actually mediates our worship.
4. He leads our praise.

He also quoted Ephesians 2:17-18: "And he came and preached peace to you who were far off and peace to those who were near. For through him we both have access in one Spirit to the Father." Jesus actually preached in Ephesus. Begg explained, "How did Jesus preach in Ephesus? Through the lips of Paul. You can hear the man's voice, but you hear God's voice. That's the worship leader we need, and that's the preacher that we require."

---

3. Strong, *A Concise Dictionary*, 44.

4. Little variation in the translation of *leitourgos* exists in the popular Bible translations. Most use the term "minister," while some use "priest." The NIV uses the phrase "one who serves," which seems weak to me. To declare Jesus as simply "one who serves" puts him in the same category as every biblical servant, which he clearly supersedes. Young's Literal Translation uses "servant." The New Life Version translates the first half of verse two as, "He is the Religious Leader of that holy place in heaven which is the true place of worship." This may be the most substantial and most useful for the purposes of this book. Strong's dictionary seems to give this hint in the definition of *leitourgos*.

5. According to Block, "Steeped in the vocabulary of the First Testament cult, the author of Hebrews demonstrates that Jesus Christ's onetime sacrifice for sins has ended the priestly service (leitourgein) and committed the ultimate "liturgical" act by which we are sanctified (Heb. 10:10-12). Likewise, he is our high priest, seated at the right hand of the throne of God, a minister (leitourgos) in the sanctuary, in the true tent that the Lord has set up (Heb. 8:1-2)." Block, *For the Glory of God*, 22.

6. Begg, "Pastor, You Are Not the Worship Leader."

As the worship leader for the church, Jesus Christ can lead us faithfully to a place of worship no other leader can. What love is displayed when Christ, the object of our worship, is also the One to lead the church to himself and to God the Father! The power of this reality draws worshippers to him and builds within them deep affection for Christ. This affection is not a flippant exercise in the unbridled passions or exuberance we may display for our favorite team but deeply felt affection for the One who purchased for the church the ability to know God fully through the worship ministry of the King of kings. This is the Christ, the Son of the Living God.

JESUS: OUR BROTHER, WORSHIPPING BESIDE US

As Jesus leads us in worship, he is also a worshipper, our brother worshipping beside his saints. The writer of Hebrews notes this by quoting Psalm 22: "I will tell of your name to my brothers; in the midst of the congregation I will sing your praise." Multiple instances in scripture portray Jesus as a worshipper, both praying and singing, prior to his crucifixion. Here, we see that as he sits at the right hand of God, he not only intercedes for us as High Priest and leads us in worship but also worships God the Father with us. Intermingled with Christ's ability to save, rejoice, and love is his ability to sing over those he loves: "The LORD your God is in your midst, a mighty one who will save; he will rejoice over you with gladness; he will quiet you by his love; he will exult over you with loud singing" (Zeph 3:17). What a powerful motivator to build our affections for him! He is the Singing Savior.[7] We gladly join him as we gather as the church and worship the Triune God.

Yet, how can Jesus be our object of worship, our worship leader, and our brother worshipping with us at the same time? When my son was four years old, he asked if there were two Jesuses. His mom told him no and asked why he had asked. He said, "Because there is Jesus in heaven, and there is Jesus in your heart." Of course, his mom explained to him that Jesus could be in both places at the same time. He then asked how Jesus could get into your heart. When his mom explained, he asked Jesus to come into his heart right on the spot. Even as believers, many of us wonder how God can exist as three persons yet be one entity. We simply accept the existence of the Trinity by faith, supported by God's word. So, we can accept Jesus accomplishing these three roles simultaneously as we meet in corporate

---

7. Kidd, *With One Voice*, 117.

worship. As Reggie M. Kidd states, "Here in a nutshell is the entire glorious mystery of the New Testament. By virtue of his resurrection, Jesus is alive in such a way that he can be both 'with us' and 'for us.'"[8]

JESUS: THE PLACE OF OUR WORSHIP

Much of our understanding related to worship is connected to a place. We have spaces in our church buildings we call sanctuaries or worship centers. Many modern Christians believe that these spaces are holy and set apart, as if somehow worship can only happen in them or, at least, happens better in them. We certainly have historical precedent for this. In the Old Testament book of Exodus, we read of the tent of meeting: "Now Moses used to take a tent and pitch it outside the camp some distance away, calling it the 'tent of meeting.' Anyone inquiring of the LORD would go to the tent of meeting outside the camp" (Exod 33:7 NIV). In Exodus 35, God gave clear instructions to create a mobile tabernacle with very specific directions on how to make it and what specific materials to use. Later, in 1 Kings, God allowed Solomon to build the temple in Jerusalem. These realities created a mindset that God can only be worshipped in holy spaces.

But Jesus made some scandalous statements regarding these ideas. In John 2:18–22, we find one such statement:

> So the Jews said to him, "What sign do you show us for doing these things?" Jesus answered them, "Destroy this temple, and in three days I will raise it up." The Jews then said, "It has taken forty-six years to build this temple, and will you raise it up in three days?" But he was speaking about the temple of his body. When therefore he was raised from the dead, his disciples remembered that he had said this, and they believed the Scripture and the word that Jesus had spoken.

It took the physical evidence of Jesus rising from the dead for the disciples to understand his message. They had to see it to believe it.

In John 4, when speaking to the Samaritan woman at the well, Jesus declares, "'Woman,' Jesus replied, 'believe me, a time is coming when you will worship the Father neither on this mountain nor in Jerusalem'" (v. 21 NIV). He went on to say, "'Yet a time is coming and has now come when the true worshipers will worship the Father in the Spirit and in truth, for they

---

8. Kidd, *With One Voice*, 115.

Jesus: His Role in Congregational Worship

are the kind of worshipers the Father seeks. God is spirit, and his worshipers must worship in the Spirit and in truth'" (v. 23–24 NIV).

It is not too much to say that Jesus declared himself to be the place of worship. He compares himself to the temple, and he states that we must worship in Spirit and Truth. Of course, we know that Jesus is Spirit and Jesus is Truth. He declares in John 14:6, "'I am the way, and the truth, and the life. No one comes to the Father except through me.'" These realities draw us to him as our place of worship. He is the way that we access the Father in worship. What a joy to know the centrality of Christ in worship!

When we understand how Jesus works in our corporate worship, we can't help but be moved to deeper and deeper affection for him. That Christ worships with us and sings with his saints powerfully remodels worship, putting a fresh perspective on what happens on Sunday mornings when the church gathers to exalt the risen Christ. He is with us in the congregation, worshipping and leading us in worship; and he is also interceding for us in heaven as our High Priest, for "when the Church gathers in worship, earth and heaven converge."[9]

---

9. Kidd, *With One Voice*, 115.

4

The Monofilament Line

> Thus says the LORD: "Stand by the roads, and look, and ask for the ancient paths, where the good way is; and walk in it, and find rest for your souls.
> JEREMIAH 6:16A

SINCE THE FALL, MAN has struggled between his two natures, created in God's image and then corrupted by Satan in the Garden of Eden. The music we use in congregational worship may lead us to worship in one of two ways. Music may lead us to worship as God intended, focusing our love and affection on him through Christ Jesus as our worship leader. Or music may lead us to embrace our passions, focusing on the flesh in the moment rather than on the long-term relationship we should be building with Christ.

Theologians, ever since New Testament times, have struggled with the dual nature of man, which often boils down to understanding the distinctions between affections and passions. As we discussed earlier, affection is an act of the will, deliberate, with the aim of building a long-term relationship. Passion is more instantaneous or gut-level, resulting in intense but short-lived emotive reactions to whatever is happening in our surroundings. Scholars have divided man's soul into two parts to talk about these differences in our nature. The upper soul encompasses the heart and the mind and is associated with the affections; the lower soul is influenced by the flesh, especially the gut, and is associated with the passions. From these associations, we get phrases such as "gut reaction" and "going with my gut." Knowing the biblical foundation for worshipping with gracious and holy affections is crucial for believers. But so is knowing the evolution of the terms *affection* and *passion* to understand the impact of those changes on present-day congregational worship.

To do this, we are creating a monofilament line from the New Testament to the present to show these changes. Why a monofilament line? Because our focus here is only on the terms *affection* and *passion* as they apply to worship. Typically, when fishing, you use a monofilament line. It is a single-strand line, which is hard for the fish to see. What I am presenting in this chapter is a monofilament line of theology, looking for one word, *affections*, in the Bible and across centuries of theological studies. This study is a monofilament line because it is singular and hard to see. The references are few, and the discussions are well-hidden. In contrast, if I were doing a study on a doctrine like salvation, I would likely find evidence more easily and follow multiple lines of inquiry, like using a braided line. For example, once I went Spoonbill fishing and caught a 60-pounder. (For perspective, last year, a man caught the record Spoonbill on our lake. It weighed 164 pounds, 13 ounces!)[1] We used a 120-pound test braided line because it is so strong. The study of affections is more like a monofilament line. Even though other events have colored our current congregational worship practices, they are omitted here unless they have a clear connection to the affections or passions.

NEW TESTAMENT

Paul reminds us in several of his letters to be aware of the impact of our passions on our lives and worship. Romans 1:26–27 reiterates man's sinful nature and how God had allowed men to give themselves over to their passions. In Galatians 5:19–21, he talks about the desires of the flesh and their negative outcomes: "sexual immorality, impurity, sensuality, idolatry, sorcery, enmity, strife, jealousy, fits of anger, rivalries, dissensions, divisions, envy, drunkenness, orgies, and things like these." Notice the words he includes that we also use to describe certain strong reactions to what is happening with us and around us: "enmity, strife, jealousy, . . . anger, rivalries, dissension, . . . envy." In Philippians 3, Paul admonishes Christians to remember that "our citizenship is in heaven" (v. 20) and to "walk according to the example" (v. 17) he and the other apostles have set, an example based on Jesus Christ. He reminds us that "many . . . walk as enemies of the cross" (v. 18). For those individuals, destruction awaits, for "their god is

---

1. Hall, "Angler Snags Giant World Record Paddlefish," para. 1.

their belly, and they glory in their shame with minds set on earthly things" (v. 19). Paul exhorts Christians through the congregation at Colossae to "set your minds on things that are above, not on things that are on earth" (Col 3:2) and to "put to death therefore what is earthly in you" (Col 3:5). In Col 3:8, Paul identifies some of the things we are to refrain from: "anger, wrath, malice, slander," again strong passionate reactions to circumstances.

Instead, Paul reminds us that as Christians, we "have crucified the flesh with its passions and desires" (Gal 5:24). We are, therefore, to "walk by the Spirit" (Gal 5:16). As we "keep in step with the Spirit" (Gal 5:25), we will experience the "fruit of the Spirit . . . love, joy, peace, patience, kindness, goodness, faithfulness, gentleness, self-control." Similarly, he tells the church at Colossae to "put on then, as God's chosen ones, holy and beloved, compassionate hearts (affections), kindness, humility, meekness, and patience" (Col 3:12).

Paul's admonishments and encouragements clearly show the biblical distinctions between passion and affection. From New Testament times until the Enlightenment, theologians reinforced these meanings. Diving in to the teaching of ancient theology helps us to recognize the importance of this study.

THE PATRISTIC FATHERS

The early Christian theologians, known collectively as the patristic fathers, were those men who preached, taught, and wrote about the message of Christ during the first five centuries. Their influence began after the death of John, the last apostle, and lasted until approximately AD 450. Their teachings and writings shaped the church, solidifying the teachings of the apostles in a time when heresies and incorrect understandings were rampant. Many of the doctrines we take for granted in evangelical churches today were still being debated and shaped over the course of these five centuries.[2] These were the men God used to ensure the church survived and

---

2. According to Cross and Livingstone, "The first Oecumenical Council, summoned by the Emp. Constantine within a few months of his conquest of the E. provinces, primarily to deal with the Arian Controversy... The Council, which had been orig. convened to Ancyra, assembled at Nicaea (now Iznik) in Bithynia in the early summer of 325 (traditionally 20 May).... The number of bishops who attended the Council is not known, since the signature lists are defective. The traditional number, which goes back to a late writing of Athanasius (Ep. ad Afros, 2), is 318, probably a symbolic figure, based on the number of *Abraham's servants (Gen. 14:14). Between 220 and 250 is more likely.

thrived. They relied on scripture, the teachings of Jesus and the apostles, and the Holy Spirit to guide them in advancing the kingdom of Christ.

The patristics viewed passions and affections as "inclinations and aversions of the soul."[3] Accordingly, they believed that we must control the passions, which can lead to sinfulness if left unchecked. They viewed God as transcendent, capable of being both impassible and deeply compassionate at the same time. They also held that affections have their source in the mind or the inner man and must be tamed through grace. The affections allow Christians to show love toward Christ and others properly.

Clement of Alexandria (AD 150–215), Nemesius of Emesa (c. AD 390), and Gregory of Nyssa (AD 335–395) recognized the distinction between the affections and passions.[4] Clement indicated that "passion is an excessive appetite" or "appetite unbridled and disobedient to the word": "Passions, then, are a perturbation (agitation) of the soul contrary to nature."[5] Clement contended that "humans should live in accordance with their nature, but passions draw them away."[6] Nemesius believed that "passion is a movement of the irrational soul."[7] Gregory believed that the passions were those properties shared with plants and animals. In sum, they reflected the irrational nature.[8] Stating that "whatever was added to human nature from the irrational life was not in us before humanity fell into passion,"[9] he also held that the passions were a result of the Fall.

As one of the "two pillars of classical Christian psychology,"[10] Augustine of Hippo (AD 354–430) shared this perspective but also went deeper, advocating for believers to exhibit appropriate godly affections. He warned "against the dangers of the passions (especially lust and anger)."[11] He also provided an understanding of man's spiritual soul, drawing a comparison

The Council, however, became generally known as 'the synod of the 318 Fathers.'" Cross and Livingstone, *The Oxford Dictionary of the Christian Church*, 1151.

3. Martin, *Understanding Affections*, 31.
4. Martin, *Understanding Affections*, 32.
5. Clement of Alexandria, *The Stromata, or Miscellanies*, Book II.
6. Martin, *Understanding Affections*, 37.
7. Nemesius of Emesa, "Of the Nature of Man," 349.
8. Martin, *Understanding Affections*, 33. Martin continues this dialogue by combining Clement, Nemesius, and Gregory into a collective thought, making their beliefs clear that the passions were unnatural and not in keeping with ordinate affections.
9. St. Gregory of Nyssa, *The Soul and Resurrection*, 114.
10. Dixon, *From Passions to Emotions*, 26. St. Thomas Aquinas is the other.
11. Dixon, *From Passions to Emotions*, 27.

to air. Although noting that the soul and air are dissimilar in many ways, he drew on their likeness, stating "that the immaterial soul is illumined with the immaterial light of the simple wisdom of God, as the material air is irradiated with material light."[12] He also noted that just as the air becomes dark in the absence of light, "so the soul, deprived of the light of wisdom, grows dark."[13]

Augustine reminded us that God, "the most exalted Creator of all, . . . had given us a mind as well as a natural reason."[14] He believed that "the soul has both lower and higher powers" (i.e., the upper and lower soul) and that the lower soul "must be subject to the higher [the upper] soul."[15] The lower soul is home to the passions, including sensation, imagination, and sense memory. The upper soul is home to two different yet related parts that, together, form the affections.[16] One part of the upper soul deals with rational knowledge that allows us to understand the temporal world. The other and highest part of the soul is the part for which God created the soul: to contemplate the divine or eternal truth. Together, the two functions of the upper soul constitute the inner man.[17]

What Augustine refers to as affections or the inner man, then, is what scripture refers to as the "heart." Moses's instructions to the Israelites illustrate this: "And now, Israel, what does the LORD your God require of you, but to fear the LORD your God, to walk in all his ways, to love him, to serve the LORD your God with all your heart and with all your soul" (Deut 10:12). From the expressions of the upper soul, then, we are able to articulate and demonstrate our love for Christ and to Christ. We are also to exhibit "proper Godly affections of sympathy, compassion, hatred of sin and so on."[18]

---

12. Aurelius Augustine, *City of God*, 489.

13. Aurelius Augustine, *City of God*, 489.

14. Augustine of Hippo, *The Trinity*, 458–59.

15. Augustine of Hippo, *City of God*, 425.

16. Martin continues: "On the other hand, the rational knowledge of earthly things, *scientia* makes right knowledge of the temporal world possible. *Sapientia*, on the other hand, is the highest power of the soul, and that for which the soul was created; *sapientia* contemplates divine or eternal truth. These two powers comprise the *mens*, or the inner man." Martin, *Understanding Affections*, 38. See Hill, Foreword to Books IX–XIV of *The Trinity*, 258–59.

17. Martin, *Understanding Affections*, 38.

18. Dixon, *From Passions to Emotions*, 27.

For the patristic fathers, affections and passions are quite distinct from each other, although both are seated in the soul. Passions are a movement of man's sense appetite toward the temporal world, which must be strictly controlled by reason (upper soul). If left uncontrolled, passions lead to sinfulness. Affections have their source in the mind or inner man and must be disciplined through grace, as indicated in Ephesians 2:8–9: "For by grace you have been saved through faith. And this is not your own doing; it is the gift of God, not a result of works, so that no one may boast." The affections allow us to express our love for Christ and others properly.

THE MEDIEVAL THEOLOGIANS

The Middle Ages began with the final fall of the Western Roman Empire in AD 476. Because of the lack of a centralized government, little documentation of what occurred during the first part of this period, known as the Dark Ages, exists. The lack of a centralized government also led to the further expansion of the church. Medieval theologians continued to build upon the thoughts and teachings of the patristic fathers and "perpetuated the distinction between movements of the soul's higher and lower faculties."[19] Three medieval theologians were significant in their contributions to the church's understanding of the affections, making deeper and finer distinctions: Anselm of Canterbury (AD 1033–1109), Bernard of Clairvaux (AD 1090–1153), and Thomas Aquinas (AD 1225–1274).

Anselm clearly articulated a distinction between affection and passion. He went to great lengths to perpetuate the belief that one's affections should develop. Referring to "his book of prayers as an aid to 'stir up the affections to prayer,'"[20] he declared in his first meditation that we are "to establish thy heart's affections in the strength of Christ."[21] Anselm believed God was both impassable (passionless) and compassionate, concluding that "God is compassionate, in terms of our experience, because we experience the effect of compassion. God is not compassionate, in terms of his own being,

---

19. Martin, *Understanding Affections*, 46.

20. Martin, *Understanding Affections*, 46.

21. St. Anselm states, "When by penance, by confession, by tears, by carefully inviting holy thoughts into the heart, thou hast clean escaped, then beware that thou fall not back: but from the deep of thy heart of hearts sigh thou in the sight of God, and implore his mercy that He would set thy feet upon the rock; ask him, that is to say, to establish thy heart's affections in the strength of Christ." St. Anselm, *Book of Meditations and Prayers*, 25–26.

because he does not experience the feeling (*affectus*) of compassion."[22] This compassion from God does not result in an affection felt by God but rather in God's compassion being felt by man. In effect, God draws us deeper and wider in our faith.

Bernard of Clairvaux, the writer of the hymn "Jesus, the Very Thought of Thee," not only emphasized affection for God but also distinguished between the "intellect and affections," mirroring the four categories of passions that Augustine identified: "distress, joy, fear, and desire." He, too, separated the passions and the affections, ascribing the passions to the lower soul and "the affections with the will."[23]

Going deeper, Bernard identified four degrees of love by which we ascend to pure love for God. The first degree is carnal or natural love, the love we have for ourselves for our own sake. This kind of love leads to social love, which is the love of our neighbors. Social love eventually leads us to the second degree of love: loving God for our own benefit.[24] To this degree, we are interested in God because of what he can do for us. However, for those of us truly seeking God, this second degree leads us to understand that love for God is possible only through God's grace.[25] As we keep seeking, we move into the third degree of love: loving God for God's own sake, loving him simply because he is God and not because of what he can do for us. With this type of love, we begin to build a real relationship with God. Most of us who reach this level stay here.

Attaining the fourth degree, loving ourselves for God's own sake, is rare and may be momentary. Yet, it is the level God intends all creation to experience. The fourth degree is the apex of love that results in divine grace and the replacement of our will with God's will. Such love is possible only through God's strength: "In him should all our affections center, so that in all things we should seek only to do his will, not please ourselves."[26]

Reaching the highest level of love for God is only available through God's strength. At this level of love, we are completely free as we lose ourselves in God, "as though we did not exist, utterly unconscious of ourselves and emptied of ourselves. . . . We will be of one mind with God, and our

---

22. St. Anselm, *Basic Writings*, 13.

23. Martin, *Understanding Affections*, 47.

24. One of the men in my discipleship class referred to this kind of love as "fire insurance," getting saved to avoid hell.

25. Bernard of Clairvaux, *On Loving God*, 38.

26. Bernard of Clairvaux, *On Loving God*, 43.

wills in one accord with God."²⁷ We don't just live our lives for God but let God be our lives. Elaborating on the fourth degree, Bernard stated that "for even an instant to lose thyself, as if thou wert emptied and lost and swallowed up in God, is no human love, it is celestial."²⁸

Bernard also identified three grades of love: carnal, rational, and spiritual.²⁹ Carnal love refers to worldly or fleshly love, loving the things of this world, passions. Rational love is more self-controlled and based on sound thought and choice; it grows more slowly. Spiritual love is selfless love. It occurs when we take our focus off ourselves and focus on others, not expecting any benefit in return. As human beings, we may experience all three grades of love.

In terms of our love and affection for God, we need to move toward spiritual love. Carnal love is counter to the Christian faith, yet even the disciples directed carnal love toward Jesus, often in response to his trying to prepare them for his coming crucifixion (Matt 16:22–23). When they reacted in carnal love, he rebuked them. By showing that even the most deeply spiritual individuals may love God carnally, we see that worshipping Jesus wrongly is possible and maybe even probable. Yet Bernard indicated that loving God carnally was still better than loving the world. We can grow from that kind of love toward a "higher love for Christ."³⁰

Thomas Aquinas was one of the most brilliant theologians of the medieval period. Living toward the end of the Middle Ages (AD 1225–1274), he built his writings upon the theological shoulders of the patristic fathers, especially Augustine. His works, including *Summa Theologiae* and *Summa Contra Gentiles*, influenced all subsequent theology.³¹ Here, however, the focus is on his position regarding affection and passion.

Although more complex than Augustine's views, Aquinas also "differentiated between rational intellect and the will on the one hand and irrational lower appetites on the other."³² Rational intellect and the will were preferable to the lower appetites; and, between the intellect and the will, intellect was superior. For both Augustine and Aquinas, "the passions were signs of deficiency and imperfection . . . contrasted unfavorably with

---

27. Foster, "The Four Degrees of Love," 40.
28. Bernard of Clairvaux, *On Loving God*, 42.
29. Bernard of Clairvaux, *On Loving God*, 42.
30. Bernard of Clairvaux, *On Loving God*, 49.
31. Dixon, *From Passions to Emotions*, 35.
32. Dixon, *From Passions to Emotions*, 42.

the cognitive powers of the soul."[33] Aquinas believed that the soul existed by itself and that the combination of the soul and the body formed the human person. He held that to understand human emotions, we have to understand the soul. From the soul, then, man can be affectionate toward God: "We draw near to God by no corporeal (bodily) steps, since He is everywhere, but by the affections of our soul." [34]

THE REFORMERS

Following the Middle Ages came the Renaissance (AD 1300–1600). This period of "rebirth" saw great growth in culture (art, architecture, literature, science), the rise of humanism, and emphasis on both political and religious freedoms. Developing slowly from the end of the Middle Ages, the Reform movement emerged in northern Europe, creating radical change in church life for believers. Prior to the Reformation, going to church entailed sitting in church and being read scripture, usually in a language most of the congregants did not know, and following the prescribed rites and rituals led by the priest. No one owned a Bible and very few could read even if they had Bibles, so they had no way of diving deeply into the word. With the Renaissance, however, came the printing press and a greater emphasis on education. These and other changes led to splits within the church, with southern Europe remaining essentially Roman Catholic in belief and northern Europe developing various Protestant sects. The most notable moment of the Reformation may have been Martin Luther's publication of his *Ninety-Five Theses*, aimed at correcting many of the corrupt practices that had developed in the church. This event is often deemed the start of the Reformation, although the shifts had been progressing over the centuries.

Here, we focus on the theology of affection that had grown from the New Testament era through the Reformation. Despite a variety of specific understandings related to word usage, theologians throughout these historical periods held the consistent view that godly believers should have a deep affection for the Lord and should avoid the inordinate passions that would cause them to focus on worldly pleasures.

The Reformers emphasized that the heart was the seat of man's affections. Although this focus built upon the path of the New Testament, patristic, and medieval writers, the Reformers redirected their understandings

---

33. Dixon, *From Passions to Emotions*, 42.
34. Aquinas, *Summa Theologica*, STh., Iq.3 a.1 ad5

away from global concepts to an emphasis on the individual, personal, and total depravity of man. However, two key theologians during the Reformation, Philipp Melanchthon (AD 1497–1560) and John Calvin (AD 1509–1564), maintained a connection with traditional Christian understandings of human affections. Both viewed affections as "inclinations or aversions" that were "closely connected to the will."[35]

Melanchthon emphasized the role of faith in developing affection for Christ. He considered man's "will and affections" to be "by nature wholly corrupt and confused"; therefore, the only path to higher affections that honor God is through genuine faith in Christ.[36] He defined faith itself as an affection of the heart that "clings to the promises and threatenings [fear] of God." However, he distinguished between mere intellectual assent and sincere faith. We can't derive faith only from head knowledge because "true faith in Christ stills the heart and moves the believer to thankfulness and good works."[37] For Melanchthon, then, our affections for Christ grow out of true faith in Christ.

Calvin is most noted for the doctrinal belief named for him, Calvinism, which holds firmly to the doctrine of election and God's ultimate sovereignty in salvation. On many points, his understanding of human affections resonates with Melanchthon. Calvin divided the soul into two parts: the mind ("understanding") and the heart ("dispositions and wills").[38] He believed that genuine affection for God is essential for true piety and salvation; reason alone cannot bring us to God. We "cannot even begin to approach God" unless we have "heart affections" for him.[39] We receive such affections by the power of the Holy Spirit. Calvin built upon the Apostle Paul's teaching in Romans 12:2 and Ephesians 4:20–24, calling for believers to continually renew their minds:

> It is, indeed, true that if we had quiet and composed minds ready to learn, the final outcome would show that God always has the best reason for his plan: either to instruct his own people in patience, or to correct their wicked affections and tame their lust, or to subjugate them to self-denial, or to arouse them from

---

35. Martin, *Understanding Affections*, 66.
36. Martin, *Understanding Affections*, 60–61.
37. Martin, *Understanding Affections*, 62.
38. Martin, *Understanding Affections*, 63.
39. Martin, *Understanding Affections*, 64.

sluggishness; again, to bring low the proud, to shatter the cunning of the impious and to overthrow their devices.[40]

As a result of renewing their minds, believers with genuinely pious hearts can forgo affections for worldly things.

Calvin also viewed affections as being of two types: inclinations and aversions. Inclinations were those affections drawing us toward Christ; aversions were those things drawing us away. However, Calvin often caused confusion by using the terms *affections* (*affectus*) and *passions* (*passione*) synonymously. To clarify, he distinguished between "higher and lower movements."[41] True believers should avoid lower movements and feed higher movements or affections.

The Reformers held that all human affections and passions are corrupt by nature. They believed that man is totally corrupt without faith in Christ empowered by the Holy Spirit. However, through the power of the Spirit and through genuine faith in Christ, man can have his affection for Christ grow; and in that strength, he can and should allow his affection for Christ to overcome his passions for a sinful world.

THE ENLIGHTENMENT

The Enlightenment or Age of Reason began in the seventeenth century and lasted through the Napoleonic wars (c. AD 1601–1815). This intellectual movement encouraged the use of reason to make sense of the world, espousing the "concept of a world of calculable regularity . . . seemingly prov[ing] that rigorous mathematical reasoning offered the means, independent of God's revelations, of establishing truth."[42] From this period evolved the "first modern secularized theories of psychology and ethics,"[43] including the firm establishment of the term *emotion* to signify any feeling.[44]

In terms of religion, the Enlightenment moved us from a God-centered worldview to an individual, human-centered worldview. The religious movement emanating from the use of reason was Deism, which believed that (1) God existed but was essentially an "architect" or a "mechanism," (2)

---

40. Calvin, *Institutes of the Christian Religion*, 211.
41. Martin, *Understanding Emotions*, 65.
42. Duignan, "Enlightenment: European History," para. 3.
43. Duignan, "Enlightenment: European History," para. 1.
44. Online Etymology Dictionary, "emotion."

God had a system of rewards and punishments he applied to human beings, and (3) people were to be virtuous and pious.[45]

However, during the early part of this era, most theologians still held a view of the lower and higher affections and a view of the bodily passions. Despite a variety of specific understandings and semantic issues related to word usage, the consistent view was that godly believers should have a deep affection for the Lord and avoid the passions that would cause them to focus on worldly pleasures. Of the many well-known theologians and philosophers of this period, two are most notable in terms of the shift in understanding of affections and passions that occurred: Rene Descartes (AD 1596–1650) and Blaise Pascal (AD 1623–1662).

Descartes wrote *The Passions of the Soul* in the early stages of the Enlightenment, introducing new perspectives on the passions and affections and a new, radically different understanding of the soul. He approached the subject from the perspective of "natural philosopher rather than moral philosopher."[46] He believed that "the passions are 'perceptions or sensations or excitations of the soul which are referred to it in particular and which are caused, maintained and strengthened by some movement of the spirits.'"[47] Furthermore, "the passions move upon the soul via the animal spirits (themselves corporeal movements), and the soul controls the body via the 'pineal' gland near the center of the brain."[48] Scientists no longer agree with this analysis.

Nevertheless, Descartes's perspective changed the conversation. Moving beyond anything the previous group of theologians and philosophers could have accepted, he did not see any godly or Christian influence in a person's life. Instead, all life is a struggle between the will and the passions. While hope exists that the will can win the battle, no spiritual resources exist to help the will succeed. Yet Descartes also believed the will is morally superior to the passions. This fundamental shift also eliminated the accepted meanings of the "higher and lower soul," changing the usage of the terminology involved.[49]

---

45. Duignan, "Enlightenment: European History," para. 1.

46. Martin, *Understanding Affections*, 67.

47. Martin, *Understanding Affections*, 67.

48. Martin, *Understanding Affections*, 67–68. For more, see Descartes, *Passions of the Soul*.

49. Martin, *Understanding Affections*, 68.

Blaise Pascal was a brilliant mathematician, scientist, and philosopher. He took a moderated view of human passions and affections, "emphasiz[ing] the morality of love and passions in continuity with the Christian theology,"[50] as seen in this passage from *Pascal's Pensées*:

> Abraham took nothing for himself, but only for his servants. So the righteous man takes for himself nothing of the world, nor the applause of the world, but only for his passions, which he uses as their master, saying to the one, "Go," and to another, "Come." The passions thus subdued are virtues. Even God attributes to himself avarice, jealousy, anger; and these are virtues as well as kindness, pity, constancy, which are also passions. We must employ them as slaves, and, leaving to them their food, prevent the soul from taking any of it. For, when the passions become masters, they are vices; and they give their nutriment to the soul, and the soul nourishes itself upon it, and is poisoned.[51]

This perspective on affections is helpful because

> God most desires humanity's affections; therefore, when individuals attach "sovereign love" to created things they commit the most grievous of sins. Hence Scripture's proofs appeal not to the mind, but to the heart, the seat of charity. The "zeal of charity" can destroy affections for the world.[52]

Thus, Pascal provides a hybrid view that opens the discussion to a post-Enlightenment world. Understanding the affections is complicated and difficult, but Pascal shows understanding them is an unrelenting and important need in the modern world given the changing nature of the definitions and people's current perceptions about affections.

From the New Testament age through the Reformation, a period of over fourteen hundred years, our monofilament line shows that the understanding of the affections and passions had remained fairly consistent. With the Enlightenment, however, came significant changes to Christianity that still reverberate today. Both Descartes and Pascal successfully changed the psychological understanding of humanity, fundamentally transforming the conventional wisdom regarding passions and affections.[53] Man rather

---

50. Martin, *Understanding Affections*, 69.
51. Pascal, *Pascal's Pensées*, 215.
52. Martin, *Understanding Affections*, 70.
53. Martin, *Understanding Affections*, 73.

than God became the focus, with affections and passions understood as purely psychological terms.[54]

However, the Enlightenment also led to a religious backlash that began in the British colonies in North America, the Great Awakening (AD 1720–1750). This period profoundly affected our understanding and use of the terms *affections* and *passions* in ways that continue to affect our congregational worship services today.

---

54. According to Martin, "By the time of the Puritans and the Reformed Scholastics, the affections were seen as the positive movements of the soul, often in connection with the will. By definition, a genuine believer has a will and affections bent toward God. Because humanity is utterly depraved, changed affections could only come through God's grace and the regenerating work of the Spirit of God. People are unable in themselves to change their will toward God. Following the teaching of Calvin and Melanchthon, faith included changed affections or inclinations toward the Triune God and away from sin. As time went on, more and more attention was given to the problem of counterfeit affections. Professing believers would show signs of having such changed affections, but they would eventually reveal themselves to be mere hypocrites." Martin, *Understanding Affections*, 89.

5
Gracious and Holy Affections (Light with Heat) Part 1

> Though you have not seen him, you love him. Though you do not now see him, you believe in him and rejoice with joy that is inexpressible and filled with glory.
> 1 Peter 1:8

As I shared in the introduction, I first encountered the phrase, "set your affections on Jesus Christ," in 1989. It simmered in my heart until, in 2016, I had a professor explain the distinction that Jonathan Edwards made between passions and affections. This understanding revolutionized my perspective on worship, which is the reason I've committed three chapters in this book to a study of Edwards's significant treatise *Religious Affections*. My hope is that doing so will revolutionize your perspective on worship as well.

In *Religious Affections*, Edwards laid the foundation for understanding what was happening in eighteenth-century New England. His purpose was to attempt to clarify the church's understanding of the conversion experiences of those swept up in the First Great Awakening that was taking place in his day. A variety of opinions existed concerning what was happening during this significant spiritual, historical, and cultural event when many were coming to faith in Christ. In attempting to give an interpretation of this event, Edwards focused particularly on the dramatic way in which some individuals were coming to Christ. In his treatise, Edwards set out to "show the distinguishing marks of a work of the Spirit of God,"[1] a massive

---

1. Edwards, *Religious Affections*, 7.

Gracious and Holy Affections (Light with Heat) Part 1

endeavor and high-end challenge for any writer, even one as revered as Edwards. He developed the work in three parts. Part 1 addresses the importance of gracious affections in true religion. Part 2 addresses twelve signs indicative of no gracious affections ("signs of nothing"[2]). Part 3 addresses twelve signs indicative of genuine gracious affections. His basis for the treatise came directly from the word of God: "Whom having not seen, ye love; in whom, though now ye see him not, yet believing, ye rejoice with joy unspeakable and full of glory" (1 Pet 1:8 KJV).[3] The ESV version reads, "Though you have not seen him, you love him. Though you do not now see him, you believe in him and rejoice with joy that is inexpressible and filled with glory." Edwards referenced the verses that precede and follow 1 Peter 1:8, indicating that those verses refer to trials that will often impact the Christian life. In writing *The Worship Target*, my desire is to bring forward the teaching of Jonathan Edwards so that his understandings of gracious affections are accessible to the modern reader.

Edwards claimed that trials provide three benefits to true Bible-believing Christians. First, trials aid in distinguishing between a true faith and a false faith. Second, they cause genuine beauty and gentleness to appear. Third, they tend to purify and increase one's true religion or genuine biblical faith. Thus, "as gold that is tried in the fire . . . becomes more solid and beautiful . . . so true faith being tried . . . becomes more precious, and thus also is found unto praise, and honor, and glory."[4] These three benefits result in two exercises of true religion. First is the evidence of a love to Christ. Second is the evidence of a joy in Christ. Edwards based his twelve signs of genuine gracious affections on these benefits and exercises of a truly biblical Christian life.

Following the discussion in part 1 of the importance of gracious affections in true religion, Edwards discussed twelve signs in part 2 that indicate no certain gracious affections. In other words, he provided twelve signs of nothing. These signs may accompany gracious affections, or they may accompany extreme passion or psychological outbursts. The point of part 2 is to show that certain, mostly physical, expressions are not sure signs of anything. Therefore, putting too much value on these signs is unwise. In part 3, Edwards addressed the twelve signs of gracious affections, the signs of true biblical faith: (1) the spiritual, supernatural, and divine; (2)

---

2. Storms, *Signs of the Spirit*, 59.
3. Edwards, *Religious Affections*, 8.
4. Edwards, *Religious Affections*, 8.

the transcendence and the amiable nature of Christ; (3) the loveliness and moral excellency of God; (4) exclusion of any focus on heat without light; (5) spiritual conviction; (6) evangelical humiliation; (7) a change of nature; (8) a Christlike and lamblike temper; (9) a Christian temper; (10) symmetry; (11) a spiritual appetite and hunger for more; and (12) fruit in Christian practice.

The focus of this book is to encourage the church and its leadership to target the gracious affections in worship instead of targeting the passions. During the late twentieth and early twenty-first centuries, a widespread attempt to target a passionate response in congregational worship has emerged. This appeal to be passionate in worship has come from preachers and from worship leaders, as well as national organizations and worship artists.[5] As a worship leader, I had a season where I bought into the concept that a physical response indicated true worship. I believed that if the congregation spontaneously stood to their feet, clapped to the music, raised their hands, or exercised any other number of physical responses, then I had been successful. The key concept here is the targeting of the passions. The goal is to energize the worshipper's physical response instead of any attempt to incline the will toward an affectionate response to Christ. According to Ryan J. Martin, "Christian churches, in the name of Jesus Christ, habitually exploit the appetites and passions to win converts."[6]

Although passions are not necessarily a bad result of worship, they should not be the target. Targeting the passions in worship asks very little of the congregant as this approach to singing in worship relegates the work of worship to those on the platform, allowing those in the congregation to simply be caught up in the euphoria. Instead, worship pastors should target the gracious affections in worship; and, if the result is a passionate response, then so be it.

Many believe that the affections should control the passions. According to Samuel Clarke,[7] "he ought to bridle his appetites, with temperance;

---

5. Outgrowths of this movement are the Passion Conference, a large-scale event that tours the United States, and Passion Music, produced by the same group. This is not to say that everything that Passion produces is wrong, but it is surprising that a worship company would choose this name while scripture in general exhorts us to "flee youthful passions" (2 Timothy 2:22).

6. Martin, *Understanding Affections*, 237.

7. Yenter and Vailati state, "Samuel Clarke (1675–1729) was the most influential British metaphysician and philosophical theologian in the generation between Locke and Berkeley and only Shaftesbury rivals him in ethics." Yenter and Vailati, "Samuel Clarke," para. 1.

to govern his passions, with moderation; and to apply himself to the business of his present station in the world, whatsoever it be, with attention and contentment."[8] The variety in Edward's focus serves as a blessing both for the church and worship leadership because through these twelve signs of gracious and holy affections, Christians may understand better what it means to have truly gracious and holy affection for Christ.

Targeting gracious affections will allow the church to focus on Christ in worship and believers' deep-seated affection for him. The worship service in any church is its largest discipleship group. Therefore, the church's leaders should be discipling their members to grow in their gracious affection towards Christ.

My goal each Sunday is to target a growing affection for Christ in congregational worship. Recently, we had a spectacular day in our Sunday worship service. The songs were deeply theological (I even called it a theological treatise of worship music), and the congregation was engaged in worship. At the Monday morning staff meeting, my pastor teased me a bit by saying, "It got a little passionate yesterday!" My response was, "That's the great thing about targeting the affections, you will often get both!" The problem is that when you target the passions, they are so overwhelming that may be all that you get.

The following sections of this chapter and the next each focus on one of the twelve signs, with the eighth and ninth signs considered together due to their similarities. The goal in these descriptions and analyses is threefold. First, by updating the language Edwards used in "Distinguishing Signs of Truly Gracious and Holy Affections," you may connect with Edwards's teaching. To this end, I have quoted each sign in its original eighteenth-century English form and have provided a more modern English version. Second, through focusing the discussion on the application of each of the signs on congregational worship and, more specifically, congregational singing, readers may adjust the target of congregational singing so that they may lead their churches in growing gracious affections toward Christ. Third, through focusing on the Bible passages that Edwards references in his writing, readers may strengthen their convictions that targeting the affections in worship is a worthy goal.

---

8. Clarke, *A Discourse concerning the Unchangeable Obligations*, as quoted in Dixon, *From Passions to Emotions*, 95.

THE FIRST SIGN: SPIRITUAL

In Edwards's own words, "Affections that are truly spiritual and gracious, do arise from those influences and operations on the heart, which are spiritual, supernatural, and divine."[9] In other words, spiritual affections that are full of grace grow from godly influences on the heart. Martin noted that "holy affections were absolutely supernatural."[10] In using the term *spiritual*, Edwards was referring to those persons who are "sanctified by the Spirit of God."[11] This sanctification results in them being set apart, distinct from both the carnal man and the natural man. He further cited these characteristics of the spiritual man:

1. He is in opposition to carnal man.
2. He is sanctified and gracious and has a spiritual mind (Rom 8:6–7).
3. He has spiritual wisdom (Col 1:9), spiritual blessings (Eph 1:3), and a relationship to the Holy Ghost or the Spirit of God.

The Spirit of God residing in a man is what makes him spiritual; and because he is spiritual, he can grow in his gracious affections for Christ.

Worship leaders, pastors, praise team members, choir members, and others should be spiritual people. They should be seeking God on a regular basis by spending time in his word, praying, and worshipping privately. Do we honestly believe we can accomplish spiritual things on the stage if we haven't done so in our prayer closet? I'm grateful for a wife who sets the standard for me. Every morning, while putting on her makeup, she is listening to a sermon by godly expositors of the word. She follows that up with her quiet time in the word and prayer. We should all prepare our hearts daily to celebrate with the congregation on Sunday. Gracious affections grow out of a truly spiritual relationship with God guided by the power of the Spirit of God.

The carnal or natural man, on the other hand, does not receive the things of God and cannot know the things of God. He is ungodly and has no grace: "For certain people have crept in unnoticed who long ago were designated for this condemnation, ungodly people, who pervert the grace of our God into sensuality and deny our only Master and Lord, Jesus Christ" (Jude 4). According to Edwards, the word translated here as "sensual" is the

---

9. Edwards, *Religious Affections*, 72.
10. Martin, *Understanding Affections*, 234.
11. Edwards, *Religious Affections*, 72.

same word translated as "natural" (man) in 1 Corinthians 2:14–15: "The natural person does not accept the things of the Spirit of God, for they are folly to him, and he is not able to understand them because they are spiritually discerned. The spiritual person judges all things but is himself to be judged by no one." In this passage, the natural man "does not accept the things of the Spirit of God."

Today, the person who leads the congregational singing in the church has a powerful and important role. Some members come to a worship gathering wanting to be entertained or to sing songs that have sentimental value to them. Others come with a deep desire to worship God by singing deeply theological songs of the faith. The leader puts theology into the voice of the congregation. As the church sings, people learn and memorize what they are singing. Although preaching the word is primary in biblical churches, church members rarely go out of the building and quote more than a few lines of any given sermon. The songs that the congregation sings, however, can become the soundtrack of church members' lives. This reality makes the worship pastor's choices incredibly important, for he must choose songs that are truly spiritual. Worship leaders must raise the bar in worship high enough to challenge those who come prepared for genuine worship. This challenge is present every time the church gathers.

Of more critical importance, however, is that worship leaders must be spiritual as well. Our target in choosing the songs for the church and in leading those songs should be to help church members grow in their gracious and holy affections towards Christ. How does the leader grow spiritually? Many books have been dedicated to this topic, and I can't fully answer this question in this space; but it seems appropriate to spend some time on this critical topic. There are four areas from which worship leaders will benefit spiritually: (1) spending time reading God's word, (2) spending time in prayer, (3) being a worshipper, and (4) guarding their hearts. I will elaborate on this in chapter 11 of the book.

THE SECOND SIGN: TRANSCENDENCE

The second sign of genuine gracious and holy affections that Edwards identified is transcendence: "The first objective ground of gracious affections, is the transcendently excellent and amiable nature of divine things as they are themselves; and not any conceived relation they bear to self, or self-interest."[12] In other words, the foundation of gracious and holy affections is to focus on God's characteristics of greatness and kindness and not on how those characteristics benefit us. Edwards declared that "the affection of love is . . . the fountain of all affections."[13] He contended that one's love for God and one's love for God's "transcendently excellent and amiable nature" will grow as one's gracious and holy affections grow. He also argued that "the divine excellency and glory of God and Jesus Christ, the word of God, the works of God, and the ways of God, etc., is the primary reason why a true saint loves these things."[14] More simply, true love for God grows not because of what he gives the believer but because of who he is. This true love is pure and will grow to the point that his happiness will grow out of his love for God. Edwards argued that this kind of love for self is the result of a true love for God and not the reverse, as our present society promotes:

> If after a man loves God, and has his heart so united to him, as to look upon God as his chief good, and on God's good as his own it will be a consequence and fruit of this, that even self-love, or love to his own happiness, will cause him to desire the glorifying and enjoying to God; it will not thence follow that this very exercise of self-love, went before his love to God and that his love to God was a consequence and fruit of that.[15]

The order of this love, then, is for one to grow deeply in love with Christ, let that affection envelop him, and then grow in love for self, allowing an even deeper love for God. However, such love must begin with a genuine affection for Christ.

As worship pastors, we may find ourselves in a quandary as we attempt to meet the needs of the congregation while being faithful to the word of God and helping the church to grow in their gracious and holy affections for Christ. In resolving this quandary, Edwards would contend that, first and foremost, worship leaders must exalt Christ in worship, holding high the transcendence and amiable nature of God and allowing Christ to draw people to himself. Once accomplished, believers' proper view of self and happiness will follow, allowing them to grow in their love for Christ even more. The Apostle Paul presented the challenge in Colossians 3:2: "Set your affection on things above, not on things on the earth" (KJV). Truly gracious

---

12. Edwards, *Religious Affections*, 95.
13. Edwards, *Religious Affections*, 95.
14. Edwards, *Religious Affections*, 95.
15. Edwards, *Religious Affections*, 95.

affections are developed in the heart, mind, and will of the believer. Musical worship should provide content in the songs of worship that challenge believers to grow in their understanding of who God the Father, God the Son, and God the Holy Spirit truly are, "to be controlled by holy affections shows the influence of the Holy Spirit."[16] The charge of the worship pastor, then, is to target the gracious affections in worship and allow God to do the work of bolstering the believers' love of self.

THE THIRD SIGN: MORAL EXCELLENCY

Growing one's affections for Christ is a gradual process, as Edwards's progression through the twelve signs shows. The third sign, moral excellency, is a clear example of each sign building on the previous signs:

> Those affections that are truly holy, are primarily founded on the loveliness of the moral excellency of divine things. Or (to express it otherwise) a love to divine things for the beauty and sweetness of their moral excellency is the first beginning and spring of all holy affections.[17]

He further stated that "this moral excellency of an intelligent being, when it is true and real . . . is holiness,"[18] claiming that no other "true virtue, but real holiness"[19] exists. He continued: "Holiness comprehends all the true virtue of a good man, his love to God, his gracious love to men, his justice, his charity, and bowels of mercies, his gracious meekness and gentleness, and all other true Christian virtues that he has, belong to his holiness."[20] Stated more simply, gracious affections are based upon a love for the holiness and moral perfection of God. Therefore, believers growing in their sanctification (holiness) as they grow in their affections for Christ is essential. Without holiness, there is no growth in gracious and holy affections: "Strive for peace with everyone, and for the holiness without which no one will see the Lord" (Heb 12:14).

Being fully aware of the level of holiness in the individuals that compose the congregations we lead in worship week after week is nearly

---

16. Martin, *Understanding Affections*, 234.
17. Edwards, *Religious Affections*, 103.
18. Edwards, *Religious Affections*, 104.
19. Edwards, *Religious Affections*, 104.
20. Edwards, *Religious Affections*, 104.

impossible. However, we can evaluate our own level of holiness and, to some degree, the holiness of those who join to form our teams. According to Edwards,

> Holy persons, in the exercise of holy affections, do love divine things primarily for their holiness: they love God, in the first place, for the beauty of his holiness or moral perfection, as being supremely amiable in itself. Not that the saints, in the exercise of gracious affections, do love God only for his holiness; all his attributes are amiable and glorious in their eyes; they delight in every divine perfection; the contemplation on the infinite greatness, power, knowledge, and terrible majesty of God, is pleasant to them.[21]

This should be the expectation for all of us who lead worship in the church.

In addition, "a holy love has a holy object."[22] Worship leaders should convey this holy love for God, who is our holy object. Revelation 4:8 challenges believers to worship Almighty God who is truly holy: "And the four beasts had each of them six wings about him; and they were full of eyes within: and they rest not day and night, saying, 'Holy, holy, holy, Lord God Almighty, which was, and is, and is to come.'" Martin emphasized that "for Edwards, external worship (church attendance, singing, praying, etc.) and moral duties toward others were essential to Christian piety, but 'internal worship,' the 'worship of the heart,' was foremost."[23] Challenging ourselves and our teams to grow in our gracious and, particularly, our holy affections for Christ, then, is a reasonable and important exercise for worship pastors as we lead our teams. Doing so will result in leadership teams that will honor God and bless the church.

THE FOURTH SIGN: NOT HEAT WITHOUT LIGHT

The fourth sign states, "Gracious affections do arise from the mind's being enlightened, richly and spiritually to understand or apprehend divine things."[24] Edwards elaborated that "holy affections are not heat without light; but evermore arise from the information of the understanding,

---

21. Edwards, *Religious Affections*, 105.
22. Edwards, *Religious Affections*, 105.
23. Martin, *Understanding Affections*, 157.
24. Edwards, *Religious Affections*, 111.

some spiritual instruction that the mind receives some light or actual knowledge."[25] To put this more clearly, gracious affections are truth from the word of God (light) and not simply passions caused by external stimuli (heat). Man can increase his affections through knowledge, which is the beginning of growing in the gracious and holy affections. Man's true affections are rich and spiritual; they draw him closer to Christ and deeper in his understanding of Christ and his affection for him. However, man may have affections that are not light but simply heat: "Now there are many affections which do not arise from any light in the understanding. And when it is thus, it is a sure evidence that these affections are not spiritual, let them be ever so high."[26] Such affections are modern-day passions. Passions (or affections that only involve heat) draw man into an experience where external stimuli cause an external response.

As we as believers study, receive instruction, and understand more and more of his word, our affections for him grow deeper. As we are reminded in 1 Corinthians 2:12, "Now we have received not the spirit of the world, but the Spirit who is from God, that we might understand the things freely given us by God." In contrast are those who profess their faith but never move beyond those initial exuberant emotions (heat). Their affections are not based on real understanding but are more passionate in nature, often intense but usually short-lived. Edwards clarified in a footnote that

> many that have had mighty strong affections at first conversion, afterwards become dry and wither, and consume, and pine, and die away: and now their hypocrisy is manifest; if not to all the world by open profaneness, yet to the discerning eye of living Christians by a formal, barren, unsavory, unfruitful heart and course; because they never had light to conviction enough as yet.[27]

Without delving into the word, growing in their love for Christ and in service to him, these individuals go through the motions of worship without ever really worshipping and soon completely fall away.

In relation to congregational worship, as worship pastors, we must take care that the congregational setting is filled with light and not overpowered by heat. Good musicians, whether secular or sacred, can fill the room with heat. They can target the passions of their listeners to the point of taking them rapturously up into a musical frenzy completely based on

---

25. Edwards, *Religious Affections*, 111.
26. Edwards, *Religious Affections*, 111.
27. Edwards, *Religious Affections*, 126.

heat without conveying any true light. The challenge for worship pastors who take this approach is to reflect on this question: how will this worship experience have a spiritual impact on the worshipper? If worship leaders are not providing light, then how are they any different from secular artists?

To apply this point practically involves three specific suggestions. First, worship pastors should choose music that is theologically deep. We must carefully sift through the myriad musical choices available. Second, worship pastors should select music that does not overpower the strength of the text. Doing so is a nuanced art. By taking much care, we will allow the deep theology of the lyric to shine above and beyond the beautiful music of the selections. Third, worship pastors need to focus on the congregation as the primary ensemble in the church. We can easily fall into the temptation to overwhelm the congregation with stage musicians who are fantastic at their craft, with dim lighting over the congregation while the lights are bright on the stage, and overpowering sound that downs out any attempt of the congregation to hear one another. We will get to this later, but doesn't scripture say we should be "addressing one another in psalms and hymns and spiritual songs, singing and making melody to the Lord with your heart" (Eph 5:19)? By maintaining a clear focus on congregational singing, we can target genuine, gracious, and holy affections instead of passions.

However, passions aroused in worship even when the worship leader targets the affections are not problematic. They are a natural result of worship and can be glorifying to God. As Martin stated, "People do not need theological light alone, but heat with that light."[28] The Apostle Paul supported this in Philippians 1:9: "And it is my prayer that your love may abound more and more, with knowledge and all discernment." As worship pastors, we should target the gracious affections by helping our congregations to "abound more and more, with knowledge and all discernment."

THE FIFTH SIGN: SPIRITUAL CONVICTION

The fifth sign Edwards identified states, "Truly gracious affections are attended with a reasonable and spiritual conviction of the judgement, of the reality and certainty of divine things."[29] To say this another way, genuine affections accompany a conviction of the truth of the gospel of Jesus Christ. Edwards argued that believers with truly gracious affections also have

---

28. Martin, *Understanding Affections*, 176.
29. Edwards, *Religious Affections*, 127.

deeply held convictions. They no longer waver between two opinions but have confidence in their Christian beliefs. Believers who have grown in their truly gracious and holy affections hold true to their judgments with a deep conviction. Their doubts are settled; they see the truth. Believers with less than true affections waver in their opinions and continue to have "apprehensions" regarding the truths of the faith. Edwards explained that "by a reasonable conviction, I mean, a conviction founded on real evidence."[30] Growing in gracious affections is a lifetime endeavor that requires faithfulness to the word of God and faithfulness in the hearing of biblical preaching. Through these disciplines, Christians grow in their understanding and, ultimately, in their spiritual conviction regarding the truths of the gospel.

We worship pastors hear a wide variety of opinions regarding the music and order of the congregational worship service. Hearing our choices challenged and our work criticized requires us to have thick skins. Following Edward's fifth sign of gracious affections helps with this constant challenge: "Christian doctrines are indisputably true to a saint."[31] When we plan and lead worship from deep biblical convictions and judgments, we will, first, be doing what is proper in God's sight and, second, have a reasonable explanation for the church members who challenge them. I can honestly say that in my forty years of leading worship I have never had a church member complain about the theology of the songs I have led. They have complained about the music being too loud, too soft, too contemporary, too traditional, and so forth, but not about the theology. I have to admit that I'm proud of that. Theology has always mattered deeply to me. When church members do ask worship leaders for reasons certain songs are included in the worship service, telling them that this song or that is included because we heard it on the radio recently will not carry the same weight as telling church members that the choice was based on the biblical depth that the lyrics communicate.

Matthew 16:15–16 reminds us of the power of Edwards's fifth sign. In talking with the disciples, Jesus asked "'But who do you say that I am?' Simon Peter replied, 'You are the Christ, the Son of the living God.'" Every pastoral leader who is truly gracious in his affections for Christ will answer in the same way. This level of conviction will help us lead the church in musical worship.

---

30. Edwards, *Religious Affections*, 129.
31. Martin, *Understanding Affections*, 191.

6

Gracious and Holy Affections (Light with Heat) Part 2

> In this you rejoice . . . so that the tested genuineness of your faith—more precious than gold that perishes though it is tested by fire—may be found to result in praise and glory and honor at the revelation of Jesus Christ. 1 Peter 1:6–7

I RECENTLY LISTENED TO a comedian (Nate Bargatze) joking about being dumb. He said that part of the problem was that he never read books and he thought reading was the "key to smart." He never read books because every book was "just the most words! It doesn't let up!" He thought writers should "put some blank pages in there" to let the reader get his "head above water."[1] I don't think the publisher will let me put blank pages in, but that's kind of how I feel about chapters 5 and 6 of this book. The content is intense. Originally, these two chapters were one, and I felt that you might need a break between these twelve signs. So, I hope you've taken a breath between these chapters and are ready to dive back in.

This book is asking you to think differently about a topic that you have probably already formed strong opinions about. Growing in gracious and holy affections is a lifetime endeavor that requires faithfulness to the word of God. Through these disciplines, believers grow in their understanding and, ultimately, in their spiritual convictions regarding the gospel's truth. As we progress through Edwards's twelve signs of gracious and holy affections, we continue to see how each builds or expands upon the previous

---

1. Bargatze, "Stand Up Monologue," 8:08.

signs and how together they reflect the character of believers who truly love God, seeking after him and worshipping him with gracious and holy affections.

THE SIXTH SIGN: EVANGELICAL HUMILIATION

Edwards's first five signs are powerless without the gentle reminder of the sixth sign: "Gracious affections are attended with evangelical humiliation. Evangelical humiliation is a sense that a Christian has of his own utter insufficiency, despicableness, and odiousness, with an answerable frame of heart."[2] To put it another way, genuine humility, which is caused by the realization of man's own sinfulness, accompanies gracious affections. Edwards described evangelical humiliation, which is peculiar to true saints, in these ways:

1. "Special influences of the Spirit of God, implanting and exercising supernatural and divine principles."[3]
2. "A sense of the transcendent beauty of divine things in their moral qualities."[4]
3. "A discovery of the beauty of God's holiness and moral perfection."[5]
4. "Overcoming the heart, and changing its inclination, by a discovery of God's holy beauty."[6]
5. "Men . . . are brought voluntarily to deny and renounce themselves"[7]
6. "They are brought sweetly to yield, and freely and with delight to prostrate themselves at the feet of God."[8]
7. "Wherein the excellent beauty of Christian grace does very much consist."[9]

---

2. Edwards, *Religious Affections*, 139.
3. Edwards, *Religious Affections*, 139
4. Edwards, *Religious Affections*, 139
5. Edwards, *Religious Affections*, 139.
6. Edwards, *Religious Affections*, 139
7. Edwards, *Religious Affections*, 139
8. Edwards, *Religious Affections*, 139
9. Edwards, *Religious Affections*, 140.

8. "But the essence of evangelical humiliation consists in such humility, as becomes a creature, in itself exceeding sinful, under a dispensation of grace; consisting in a mean esteem of himself, as in himself nothing, and altogether contemptible and odious; attended with mortification of a disposition to exalt himself, and a free renunciation of his own glory."[10]

The fundamental truths of evangelical humiliation are understanding that gracious affections are derived from a supernatural and divine understanding of God and his transcendent beauty, moral qualities, and holiness: "Such humility is the primary part of the Christian's self-denial."[11] This understanding will change a man's heart and inclination to the point that he will voluntarily renounce himself, prostrate himself, yield himself, and consider himself nothing before a holy God.

In thinking about this sign from the perspective of worship leaders, we should consider the individuals who compose our worship teams. Place each member of the team on a sliding scale of humility, from *Humble Servant* to *Diva*. Most worship team members naturally fall somewhere on this scale. Individuals completely on the *Humble Servant* end struggle to stand in front of hundreds of people using their art to lead out in worship. Individuals completely on the *Diva* end lead worship for all the wrong reasons and are most likely (at least from my experience) impossible to live and work with. To lead with truly gracious affections, every individual, regardless of his natural bent, must exhibit evangelical humiliation in leading the church in worship. Micah 6:8 states, "He has told you, O man, what is good; and what does the LORD require of you but to do justice, and to love kindness, and to walk humbly with your God?" Walking humbly with God is a key requirement for each member of the worship team, particularly for the pastoral leadership of the worship team. Therefore, evangelical humiliation must be at the core of the worship leadership of the church.

THE SEVENTH SIGN: CHANGE OF NATURE

Although the seventh sign seems to be something that we may assume in the Christian faith, Edwards left nothing to chance, stating, "wherein gracious affections are distinguished from others, is, that they are attended

---

10. Edwards, *Religious Affections*, 140.
11. Martin, *Understanding Affections*, 191.

with a change of nature."[12] To rephrase, radical life change will accompany genuine gracious affections. Here, Edwards stated the most fundamental Christian truth: any person who truly encounters the redeeming and merciful power of God finds that "all spiritual discoveries are transforming"[13] and "make an alteration in the very nature of the soul."[14] He explained further that "the Spirit is united to the faculties of man, to live there. Therefore holy affections last."[15] This change of nature goes beyond the here-and-now experience and the external to create a fundamental transformation in the believer from the inside out, from now to eternity. This change in one's nature is what sets apart a Christian from a non-Christian.

The Apostle Paul made this truth clear in 2 Corinthians 3:18–19: "And we all, with unveiled face, beholding the glory of the Lord, are being transformed into the same image from one degree of glory to another. For this comes from the Lord who is the Spirit." Our goal as faithful worship pastors is twofold. First, we seek Christ to do the work of regeneration in the worship services that we are privileged to lead. Second, in our worship planning, we target the growth of genuine and holy affections in the hearts of the believers who are present in congregational worship each week. Worship is not designed for the unbeliever. The unbeliever does not have the Spirit of God and therefore cannot worship God: "Only those who receive the Holy Spirit can worship God at all. It is not within the capabilities of human flesh to do this (worship)."[16] Of crucial importance for worship leaders, then, is that they plan and lead, targeting the gracious affections in those who have been changed by the beautiful gospel of Jesus Christ.

THE EIGHTH AND NINTH SIGNS: CHRISTLIKE TEMPER

Edwards's eighth and ninth signs are so closely related, that I am considering them together. The eighth sign declares,

> Truly gracious affections differ from those affections that are false and delusive, in that they tend to, and are attended with the lamb-like, dovelike spirit and temper of Jesus Christ; or in other words,

---

12. Edwards, *Religious Affections*, 157.
13. Edwards, *Religious Affections*, 157.
14. Edwards, *Religious Affections*, 157.
15. Martin, *Understanding Affections*, 192.
16. Begg, "Pastor, You Are Not the Worship Leader."

they naturally beget and promote such a spirit of love, meekness, quietness, forgiveness and mercy, as appears in Christ.[17]

The ninth sign states, "Gracious affections soften the heart, and are attended and followed with a Christian tenderness of spirit."[18] In combining the two signs to simplify them, we may say that "gracious affections" create "a spirit of love, meekness, quietness, forgiveness and mercy, as appears in Christ" and that they "soften the heart" and build a "tenderness of the spirit."

Edwards argued that such a spirit is a truly biblical and Christian temperament, supporting his argument with multiple scriptural quotations. From the Old Testament, he quoted Proverbs 17:27: "Whoever restrains his words has knowledge, and he who has a cool spirit is a man of understanding." From the Sermon on the Mount, he quoted Jesus: "Blessed are the meek, for they shall inherit the earth . . . Blessed are the merciful, for they shall receive mercy . . . Blessed are the peacemakers, for they shall be called sons of God" (Matthew 5:5, 7, 9). He also quoted the Apostle Paul from Colossians 3:12–13: "Put on then, as God's chosen ones, holy and beloved, compassionate hearts, kindness, humility, meekness, and patience, bearing with one another and, if one has a complaint against another, forgiving each other; as the Lord has forgiven you, so you also must forgive." These truths are reflective of every Christian who is truly growing in gracious and holy affections toward Christ.

The writer of Hebrews in 8:1–2 declared that Jesus is our *leitourgos*, the leader of our worship: "Now the point in what we are saying is this: we have such a high priest, one who is seated at the right hand of the throne of the Majesty in heaven, a minister in the holy places, in the true tent that the Lord set up, not man." And so, Jesus is truly the worship leader in any Bible-believing, Christian church; and worship leaders are to follow him in worship. To do so, we should seek to emulate him and all his characteristics. Edwards specifically stated we should emulate Christ's "lamblike" and "dovelike spirit." Worship leaders should exhibit this spirit not only on the platform as they lead their congregations but also in private conversations and rehearsals with worship team members, church members, and the community alike.

Martin stated what may be a challenge for any worship leader as the primary church musician: "Since Christians are being renewed into the

---

17. Edwards, *Religious Affections*, 160.
18. Edwards, *Religious Affections*, 168.

image of Jesus Christ, they should be like him, especially in meekness."[19] Excellence in worship is a goal for most of us worship leaders, which can result in our being crass and insensitive when working with volunteer musicians who do not always perform up to expected standards. If excellence is the only standard we have, we may lose the respect of our teams as we pursue excellence without truly caring about the individuals that we lead. We may be more effective when we are gentle and kind, even when perceived standards are not being met. Replacing our desire for excellence with the goal of effectiveness may allow us to be more Christlike in temper.

THE TENTH SIGN: SYMMETRY

The tenth sign from Edwards has a certain elegance to it:

> Another thing wherein those affections that are truly gracious and holy, differ from those that are false, is beautiful symmetry and proportion . . . A holy hope and holy fear go together in the saints, as has been observed from Psalm 33:18 ('Behold, the eye of the Lord is on those who fear him, on those who hope in his steadfast love') and 147:11 ('but the Lord takes pleasure in those who fear him, in those who hope in his steadfast love').[20]

In other words, gracious and holy affections have balance: joy and sorrow, comfort and mourning, and so forth. Edwards admitted that the "virtues and gracious affections of the saints in this life (may not be) perfect."[21] He gave a few reasons for this: "through the imperfection of grace, for want of proper instructions, through errors in judgment, or some particular unhappiness of natural temper, or defects in education, and many other disadvantages that might be mentioned."[22] He continued that "although believers never have perfectly proportioned affections in this life, their affections are never characterized by the 'monstrous disproportion' one observes in hypocrites."[23] With all of that being true, Edwards contended that true believers should have a spiritual balance in their gracious affections. This balance comes from the believer's sanctification. The fullness

---

19. Martin, *Understanding Affections*, 192.
20. Edwards, *Religious Affections*, 172.
21. Edwards, *Religious Affections*, 172.
22. Edwards, *Religious Affections*, 173.
23. Martin, *Understanding Affections*, 192.

of Christ in the believer strengthens this beautiful symmetry. To support this claim, Edwards quoted John 1:16: "For from his fullness we have all received, grace upon grace."

Balance is a continual challenge in church music and worship. Often the discussion stops at the point of balancing hymns and contemporary songs, fast and slow songs, or old and new songs. However, worship pastors should pay more attention to the balance of songs that build upon and grow the church's gracious and holy affections. Focusing on gracious affections allows us to draw on a wide variety of styles and time periods while building and maintaining cohesion in worship services. Focusing on the affections instead of the passions also allows us to balance our focus on the various affections. If we consider the variety that we can implement in congregational worship as we plan, we can focus on growing different affections each week and add true freshness to worship.

THE ELEVENTH SIGN: SPIRITUAL APPETITE

Edwards's eleventh sign states, "Another great and very distinguishing difference between gracious affections and others is, that gracious affections, the higher they are raised, the more is a spiritual appetite and longing of soul after spiritual attainments increased. On the contrary, false affections rest satisfied in themselves."[24] Said another way, as gracious affections grow, they develop in the believer a hunger for more. Martin asserted that "God designed religious affections to satisfy humanity's great appetites."[25] What a joy to know this truth! As believers grow in their affections for Jesus Christ, they long for more of him!

This sign is encouraging because, eventually, believers will spend eternity worshipping Christ. The continual desire for him will make the eternal journey that much more rewarding. This truth also serves as a warning to believers to evaluate their true affections. If their affections for Christ are waning, if they have lost their desire to spend time with Christ, they need to refocus on their love for him.

Edwards expounded on this truth, providing the motivation for worship leaders to lead their churches to grow in their gracious and holy affections for Christ:

---

24. Edwards, *Religious Affections*, 179.
25. Martin, *Understanding Affections*, 193.

> The more a true saint loves God with a gracious love, the more he desires to love him, and the more uneasy is he at his want of love to him; the more he hates sin, the more he desires to hate it, and laments that he has so much remaining love to it; the more he mourns for sin, the more he longs to mourn for sin; the more his heart is broke, the more he desires it should be broke the more he thirsts and longs after God and holiness, the more he longs to long, and breathe out his very soul in longings after God: the kindling and raising of gracious affections is like kindling a flame; the higher it is raised, the more ardent it is; and the more it burns, the more vehemently does it tend and seek to burn.[26]

Initially, congregants may miss the trite songs that inflame their passions; but as they grow in their truly gracious affections, the more they will desire to continue down that path.

However, making major transitions in worship requires a gentle and loving approach, much like joining traffic on an interstate highway. The merge should be thoughtful and gentle and go with the flow. If a congregation is accustomed to singing songs that inflame the passions or sentimentality, worship leaders must take great care in leading their church members to a new target in worship. Only after we build trust with the congregation can we make changes to help congregants grow in their gracious affections in worship. Changing the songs gently and slowly will allow worshippers to adjust in time. Songs that target the affections will be full of doctrinal truth that conveys the reality of the gospel of Jesus Christ. In time, the church will grow to desire this depth in worship. As they are discipled toward a new way of worshipping, worshippers' appetites will be heightened toward truly affectionate worship.

THE TWELFTH SIGN: FRUIT IN CHRISTIAN PRACTICE

In the final sign of truly gracious and holy affections, Edwards turned his attention to the exercise and fruit of the Christian life:

> Gracious and holy affections have their exercise and fruit in Christian practice—I mean, they have that influence and power upon him who is the subject of them, that they cause that a practice,

---

26. Martin, *Understanding Affections*, 193.

which is universally conformed to, and directed by Christian rules, should be the practice and business of his life.[27]

In elaborating, Edwards stated that this sign

> implies three things: 1. That [this] behavior or practice in the world be universally conformed to, and directed by Christian rules. 2. That he makes a business of such a holy practice above all things; that it be a business which he is chiefly engaged in, and devoted to, and pursues with highest earnestness and diligence: so that he may be said to make this practice of religion eminently his work and business. And 3. That he persists in it to the end of life: so that it may be said, not only to be his business at certain seasons, the business of Sabbath days, or certain extraordinary times, or the business of a month, or a year, or of seven years, or his business under certain circumstances; but the business of his life; it being that business which he perseveres in through all changes, and under all trials as long as he lives.[28]

Stated in more modern English, gracious and holy affections will result in one living a life that is full of fruit and obedience, clearly marked by the individual's affection for Christ.

Every pastor who has ever led a church has bemoaned the fact that certain members only show up at church on certain holidays or for certain seasons and that, if other activities get in the way, their time at church is expendable. Edwards powerfully challenged here that Christians should act as Christians throughout their yearly calendars and throughout their lives. Believers who have truly gracious and holy affections for Christ want to live their lives in obedience to him. They govern their personal and professional lives in accordance with his word, not just on Sundays or during certain times of the year (i.e., Easter, Christmas) or when doing so is convenient but 24/7/365, regardless of the trials they may face. However, as human beings, we may sometimes backslide or rest on our laurels rather than continuing to press onward and upward. The writer of Hebrews tells us to "hold fast the confession of our hope without wavering, for he who promised is faithful" (Heb 10:23) and to "run with endurance the race that is set before us, looking to Jesus, the founder and perfecter of our faith" (Heb 12:1b–2).

One of the greatest gifts that we worship pastors can give to our churches is faithful, consistent leadership: "For Edwards, such obedience

---

27. Edwards, *Religious Affections*, 182.
28. Edwards, *Religious Affections*, 182–83.

and holiness were universal, not only to avoid wickedness, but to obey universally God's positive commands."[29] Worship leadership in the middle of summer should be of the same quality that the church sees at Christmastime or at Easter. This type of leadership encourages the church to follow in such a way that worshippers desire to be faithful in their Christian walk and worship.

Church leadership at all levels must maintain the understanding that gracious and holy affections must come before Christian service. Pastors must remember to keep focused on the spiritual before they call people to do the practical. If pastors focus on developing gracious and holy affections in the people of their church, they will find themselves leading a group that is willing to serve.

THE POWER OF EDWARDS'S WORK

Communicating spiritual truth and analysis is a challenging endeavor. Jonathan Edwards approached the task with humility and grace. Observing and reporting on external realities that come with the Christian faith is a relatively easy task. We can observe believers singing, reading their Bibles, sharing the gospel, or loving their neighbors and conclude that these are signs of true Christian faith. Edwards refused to do so. In fact, in part 2 of *Religious Affections*, he did the exact opposite and clearly made the point that these outward manifestations are evidence of no certain gracious affections; they are evidence of nothing.

In Edwards's twelve signs of gracious and holy affections, we find a resource that forces believers to go deep and to understand what truly happens when we come to faith in Christ. Martin stated the reason behind this book and for the study of Edwards's message in *Religious Affections* succinctly in his conclusion:

> In Christ humans see God's glory. For those who believe on him, which itself is a form of consent to this excellent Christ and God, God gives the Spirit of love, who works supernatural principles of divine love in the human heart, bringing holy affections that see the glorious beauty of holiness in the Triune God. Consequentially, this is true virtue, for human beings to love the Lord their God with all their heart, soul, mind, and strength, and their

---

29. Martin, *Understanding Affections*, 193.

neighbor as themselves. True religion, in great part, consists in holy affections.[30]

In seeking to target Christian worship consistent with Edwards's twelve signs, this challenge grows.

Edwards postulated that "holy affections are not heat without light."[31] Rephrasing Edwards, we may say, "holy affections are light with heat." If we as worship pastors target only the heat, we may never find the true light. If we target the light, however, we will most assuredly find the heat. For that reason, ardent worship pastors will be wise to spend time in Edwards's writings, seeking out holy and gracious affections.

---

30. Martin, *Understanding Affections*, 238.
31. Edwards, *Religious Affections*, 111.

7

Signs of Nothing

You are judging by appearances. If anyone is confident that they belong to Christ, they should consider again that we belong to Christ just as much as they do. 2 Corinthians 10:7 (NIV)

I WAS AT A Christian convention recently, seated in an elevated section at the back of the auditorium where I could see most of the worshippers in the room. I noticed that some worshippers raised their hands and some did not. But what caught my attention was the fact that the number of raised hands significantly increased as the band got louder and the keys got higher. I would guess, based on previous experiences, that those raising their hands believed that the Holy Spirit was moving more powerfully during those moments, so they raised their hands. And, by the way, I'm not at all in the anti-hand raising group. I believe raising hands can signify surrender to Christ and can be meaningful. But that day, it seemed apparent that the band was, intentionally or not, targeting a passionate response from the crowd. We've all heard the saying in the world of entertainment that big endings get big applause. Perhaps the same is accurate regarding worship. Loud volumes and higher keys will get more people to raise their hands in worship and give the leaders the illusion of success.

Jonathan Edwards saw many physical outbursts during the Great Awakening. As a result, he analyzed the responses and concluded that not all that might appear holy is holy. In writing about the meaning of these physical responses, Edwards used *affection* and *passion* based on the meanings of those terms before the Enlightenment, which we examined in chapter 4 along the monofilament line from the New Testament through the Enlightenment. His treatise was an attempt to restore those meanings as the changes in them added to the confusion and controversy surrounding the vast numbers professing their faith during the Great Awakening revivals.

His observations led him to identify not only twelve signs that are demonstrations of truly gracious and holy affections but also twelve signs representing no certain gracious and holy affections. These are signs that people may exhibit that do not conclusively indicate the person has been saved and is growing and worshipping in gracious and holy affections toward Jesus Christ. Most of these signs are physical. They are inconclusive of authentic faith because outward appearances may or may not accurately reflect a person's true nature or convictions. Some of these signs may even accompany gracious affections. However, they may also accompany psychological outbursts or be expressions of extreme passion. Sam Storms calls these twelve signs "Signs of Nothing,"[1] which is the jargon we will use because that's precisely what they are.

THE FIRST SIGN OF NOTHING: HEIGHT

Edwards said, "It is no sign one way or the other, that religious affections are very great, or raised very high."[2] To put that in modern English, we may say that the intensity (height) of the religious affection is not a sign that the affection is truly great. Intense responses may or may not be indicative of true faith. The Bible gives several examples of such responses that come from real faith in God. The psalms, especially, tell us to "rejoice" and "shout for joy";[3] and in Luke 6:23, Jesus tells the disciples to "leap for joy." But scripture also contains examples of intense responses that are not evidence of true affection. The Israelites soon forgot God and began worshipping a golden calf, and the crowd's shouts of "hosanna" soon turned to shouts of "crucify him."[4] In 2 Corinthians 10:7 (NIV), Paul makes it clear that outward appearances are no sign of true spirituality: "You are judging by

---

1. Storms, *Signs of the Spirit*, 59.
2. Edwards, *Religious Affections*, 28.
3. See for example Pss 47:1, 71:23, 118:24.
4. See Exod 32; Matt 21:9, 27:22–23; Mark 11:9–10, 15:13–14; Luke 23:23; John 12:13, 19:6, 15.

appearances. If anyone is confident that they belong to Christ, they should consider again that we belong to Christ just as much as they do."

THE SECOND SIGN OF NOTHING: BODILY EFFECTS

Edwards said, "It is no sign that affections have the nature of true religion, or that they have not, that they have great effects on the body."[5] The modernized version may read that bodily effects of religious affection are not signs that the affection is true. Edwards believed that to some extent all affections evidence some sort of bodily response. Scripture is replete with descriptions that reflect such responses: trembling (Ps 119:120), groaning (Rom 8:36), being sick (Song 2:5), crying out (Ps 84:2), panting (Ps 38:10), fainting (Ps 84:2). However, such physical effects may have nothing to do with our affections for Christ as we may have the same kinds of responses to worldly things and situations. Then, of course, Jesus reminded us, "Do not judge by appearances, but judge with right judgment" (John 7:24). True spirituality cannot be determined by outward bodily effects.

THE THIRD SIGN OF NOTHING: TALKING

The third sign of nothing states, "It is no sign that affections are truly gracious affections, or that they are not, that they cause those who have them to be fluent, fervent, and abundant, in talking of the things of religion."[6] In other words, talking at length about spiritual things does not provide certainty that the affections are true. Many of us, believers and nonbelievers alike, have head knowledge of Jesus Christ and scripture. But head knowledge and heart knowledge are not the same. Even Satan has head knowledge of Christ. In Matthew 12:34, Jesus rebuked the Pharisees for not loving God, despite their ability to quote scripture: "'You brood of vipers! How can you speak good, when you are evil? For out of the abundance of the heart the mouth speaks.'" So, talking about scripture and religious things and quoting scripture may or may not indicate an individual's affection for Christ.

I once had a bass player show up to join our worship band. He was a good player and talked a good talk. He had been in our worship services

---

5. Edwards, *Religious Affections*, 30.
6. Edwards, *Religious Affections*, 33.

for several weeks before he approached me about playing. One Wednesday night, when he came early for rehearsal, he found a deacon and asked where he should pick up his check. Our church was not accustomed to paying our musicians, and so that was explained to him. It was the last we saw him. The outward signs were that this man loved Jesus and wanted to serve the church. But, apparently, he just saw a way to get a paycheck.

THE FOURTH SIGN OF NOTHING: OUTSIDE YOURSELF

The fourth sign states, "It is no sign that affections are gracious, or that they are otherwise, that persons did not make them themselves, or excite them of their own contrivance and by their own strength."[7] In other words, affection aroused from sources other than one's own strength is no assurance that the affection is genuine. We have affections for many things, both religious and nonreligious. Some are intentional on our part; others result from forces acting upon us. Edwards indicated some of these affections are spurred by "the operation of an invisible agent, some spirit besides their own," but that doesn't mean it is the Holy Spirit. We are bombarded by external stimuli that prompt involuntary responses from us. We are also subject to other spirits that fight to control our hearts and minds, spirits we must guard against and test to be sure we are submitting to the Holy Spirit and not some minion of Satan.[8]

The Bible is clear when it comes to false spirits. First John 4:1 warns, "Beloved, do not believe every spirit, but test the spirits to see whether they are from God, for many false prophets have gone out into the world." Jesus made this expressly clear when he said, "For false christs and false prophets will arise and perform great signs and wonders, so as to lead astray, if possible, even the elect" (Matt 24:24). We cannot know if the outward sign is genuine or not. So, we must be cautious about targeting a passionate response in worship because, while attempting to lead others to glorify Christ, we may simply be stirring a passionate experience.

---

7. Edwards, *Religious Affections*, 35.
8. See Ephesians 1:18–19; Hebrews 6:4–8.

THE FIFTH SIGN OF NOTHING: RECALLING SCRIPTURE

This sign of nothing is difficult for Bible believers to accept because we love the word of God so much and have worked hard to commit it to memory. But Edwards says that "it is no sign that religious affections are truly holy and spiritual, or that they are not that they come with texts of Scripture, remarkably brought to the mind."[9] To restate, recalling texts of scripture from memory is no sure sign that the affection is genuine.

Some of us memorize scripture easily; others of us find it quite difficult. Regardless, being able to quote scripture does not necessarily mean someone has true faith in Christ. Sometimes, we get caught up in the beauty of God's word and assume that by learning and quoting from it, we are expressing our love for Christ; but even Satan knows scripture. He often misquotes it and uses it to entrap us, just as he tried to tempt Jesus (Matt 4). Peter also warns in 2 Peter 3:16, referencing Paul's letters, that "there are some things in them that are hard to understand, which the ignorant and unstable twist to their own destruction, as they do the other Scriptures."

THE SIXTH SIGN OF NOTHING: SHOWING LOVE

The sixth sign of nothing says, "It is no evidence that religious affections are saving, or that they are otherwise, that there is an appearance of love in them."[10] In other words, showing love is not necessarily evidence of a true gracious affection. The more excellent or rare something is, the more likely it is to be counterfeited. This is true for two of the highest affections, humility and love; they can be corrupted. We can go through the motions, appearing to show love without actually embracing that affection, whether for God or for others. Matthew 24:12 reminds us that "the love of many" toward God "will grow cold." Paul also reminds us in Ephesians 6:24 that the love of Jesus Christ is "incorruptible." We can love God because he loved us first since love is one of God's character traits. Believers who genuinely love God manifest that love in obedience to his commands.

Smooth talk can be deceitful. Some may show love, but do they hold true to the actual doctrines of the faith? Paul warns us,

> I appeal to you, brothers, to watch out for those who cause divisions and create obstacles contrary to the doctrine that you have

---

9. Edwards, *Religious Affections*, 38.
10. Edwards, *Religious Affections*, 40.

been taught; avoid them. For such persons do not serve our Lord Christ, but their own appetites, and by smooth talk and flattery they deceive the hearts of the naïve. (Rom 16:17–18)

If Christians can be deceived by the love shown by an imposter, how much more can we be deceived by someone's actions in a worship service? This provides all the more reason to target genuine, deep, doctrinal worship in our churches.

THE SEVENTH SIGN OF NOTHING: MULTIPLE AFFECTIONS

Edwards's seventh sign states, "Persons having religious affections of many kinds, accompanying one another, is not sufficient to determine whether they have any gracious affections or no."[11] We might say it this way: multiple affections in one person do not prove that they are true. We express a wide variety of affections; but depending on their root, the motivation behind them, what may resemble gracious affections may actually be false. Although similar to sign 6, this sign focuses on both the quantity and quality of the affections we express.

Edwards compared the nature of man to that of a tree. If the root system and sap within the tree are healthy, the fruit it produces is healthy. If something has poisoned the root system, the tree will not yield healthy fruit and will eventually wither and die. If the songs that we sing in worship have a solid, biblical foundation, we have a far greater chance of seeing our churches bear godly fruit. We must remember that everything we do from the platform disciples those in the worship service.

Scripture compels us in Galatians 5:16–17:

> But I say, walk by the Spirit, and you will not gratify the desires of the flesh. For the desires of the flesh are against the Spirit, and the desires of the Spirit are against the flesh, for these are opposed to each other, to keep you from doing the things you want to do.

Gracious and holy affections will be consistent with the word of God and with the Spirit of God. They will endure. However, Edwards also made it clear that multiple affections may still be false:

> It is evident that there are counterfeits of all kinds of gracious affections; as of love to God, and love to the brethren, as has been

---

11. Edwards, *Religious Affections*, 41.

just now observed; so of godly sorrow for sin, as in Pharaoh, Saul, and Ahab, and the children of Israel in the wilderness.[12]

As we lead worship, or as we participate in worship, we must be careful to target a genuine and growing affection for Christ.

THE EIGHTH SIGN OF NOTHING: THE ORDER

Edwards wanted his parishioners to know that "nothing can certainly be determined concerning the nature of the affections, by this, that comforts and joys seem to follow awakenings and convictions of conscience, in a certain order"[13] Today we may say, no predetermined order of gracious affections exists that will prove they are valid. Edwards noted a prevalent belief that believers must first experience "great terrors and awakenings" (struggling with their conviction) before they receive the "comforts and joys" that come with gracious and holy affections for Christ.[14] This may seem foreign to us, but he wanted his listeners and readers to know that the order in which one's spiritual awakening happens is no sure sign of gracious and holy affections. However, he argued that, although that may be true for some, not everyone will follow this order and when that order does exist, it does not indicate true holy and gracious affections. Satan can counterfeit those affections (signs 6 and 7) and cause believers to turn away before the work of the Holy Spirit in salvation is completed, so outward signs of conversion are still not sure signs of being saved and having genuine affection for Christ.

I remember sitting in a pastoral ministries class, listening to our professor tell a story from when he was a pastor. He was trying to reach a successful businessman in the community for the church. The man could not accept the fact that he was a sinner, but he wanted to be a part of the church and he loved Christ. The man got involved in church and was very active. Later, he came to the point where he saw his sin, confessed it to Christ, and accepted the forgiveness of Jesus in his life. We may hope that the order of our affection for Christ would come in a more traditional manner, but we don't always know how God is working.

---

12. Edwards, *Religious Affections*, 41.
13. Edwards, *Religious Affections*, 44.
14. Edwards, *Religious Affections*, 47.

THE NINTH SIGN OF NOTHING: OVER COMMITTED

The ninth sign of nothing states,

> It is no certain sign that the religious affections which persons have are such as have in them the nature of true religion, or that they have not, that they dispose persons to spend much time in religion, and to be zealously engaged in the external duties of worship.[15]

Without a doubt, Edwards was a busy pastor and found himself immersed in ministry; but he did not consider that busyness to be a genuine sign of gracious and holy affections.

The modern Christian may be grateful to know that being overly committed to religious activities does not show that affections are legitimate. Although scripture clearly indicates believers should spend time reading the word, praying, singing, and being involved in the various ministries of the church, doing these things is still not an indication of a person's salvation or genuine affection for Christ. For true believers, such activities are joy, as they were for Anna, the widow Luke tells us about (Luke 2:36–37):

> And there was a prophetess, Anna, the daughter of Phanuel, of the tribe of Asher. She was advanced in years, having lived with her husband seven years from when she was a virgin, and then as a widow until she was eighty-four. She did not depart from the temple, worshiping with fasting and prayer night and day.

But works alone, regardless of their volume, do not define our state of grace.

I had a friend who had spent over a decade as a worship leader and pastor. He had served the church, led worship, and participated in evangelism and missions and was well respected. But he finally realized he did not have a genuine relationship with Christ. I later found out that he did come to genuine faith in Christ. The point, however, is that if a pastor can be actively involved in the church's activities yet not honestly know Christ, then anyone can be busy in church life and not have genuine affection for Christ.

---

15. Edwards, *Religious Affections*, 51.

THE TENTH SIGN OF NOTHING: PRAISING GOD

This non-sign is difficult for a lifelong worship leader to accept. In fact, I have made the statement that a genuine relationship with Christ is what draws us to worship. But Edwards states that "nothing can be certainly known of the nature of religious affections by this, that they much dispose persons with their mouths to praise and glorify God."[16] Praising God with one's mouth does not prove one's gracious affections. Believers in general do not criticize other believers for praising God; it's an expected behavior. But praising God and worshipping with gracious and holy affections are not synonymous. Nonbelievers in the right circumstances may also praise God and seemingly begin to worship him, as Nebuchadnezzar did after finding Shadrach, Meshach, and Abednego safe from the fiery furnace (Dan 3:28): "Nebuchadnezzar answered and said, 'Blessed be the God of Shadrach, Meshach, and Abednego, who has sent his angel and delivered his servants, who trusted in him, and set aside the king's command, and yielded up their bodies rather than serve and worship any god except their own God.'" If an ungodly king can praise God, then surely an individual or group of individuals in church can do the same. This is particularly true if they are surrounded by devout believers who are genuinely worshipping God.

The opposite is also true. A Christian may come into a worship service incapable of praising God. What do I mean by that? I remember a young lady that started attending the worship at our church and for weeks she just sat on the back row and cried. She couldn't sing. She couldn't lift her head. All she could manage was to bow her head and cry. I never got the full story; but, eventually, she actively participated in our choir and praise team. Not only did she eventually praise God, but she also led others to do the same! Outward appearances don't tell the whole story.

THE ELEVENTH SIGN OF NOTHING: BOLDNESS

As one who has encountered thousands of believers over four decades of ministry, I have seen this firsthand. In fact, those who are the boldest are the ones that tend to fizzle out and fade away. Edwards clearly saw that "it is no sign that affections are right, or that they are wrong, that they make persons that have them exceeding confident that what they experience is

---

16. Edwards, *Religious Affections*, 52.

divine, and that they are in a good estate."[17] Having the boldness that one's spiritual experience is holy does not make it so. Boldly expressing one's faith is a sign of boldness, not necessarily of salvation. Boldness is an expression of confidence, a trait many of the heroes of the Bible exhibited and one that may become part of a believer's testimony. But being bold, fearless, determined, intense, or enthusiastic in witnessing is still not a sure sign of salvation.

I've seen people come full of enthusiasm and vigor and ready to join the worship team or choir and use their boldness for the good of the kingdom. And then I've seen them go, fading away and disappearing after a time. I love to see boldness; but, more than that, I love to see believers committed to faithfully sharing the gospel and worshipping Christ with a genuine affection for him. James 1:12 lauds perseverance: "Blessed is the man who remains steadfast under trial, for when he has stood the test he will receive the crown of life, which God has promised to those who love him." Boldness is terrific, but perseverance over time is a blessing to all.

THE TWELFTH SIGN OF NOTHING: CONFIDENCE

Believers confident in their faith should be a reassuring reality, but Edwards stated that

> nothing can be certainly concluded concerning the nature of religious affections, that any are the subjects of, from this, that their outward manifestations of them, and the relation persons give of them, are very affecting and pleasing to the truly godly, and such as greatly gain their charity, and win their hearts.[18]

Just because genuine Christians believe their affections are true does not necessarily make them so. We can often fool ourselves into thinking we are worshipping with genuine affection for Christ when we aren't. We may be too focused on how others may perceive us during worship. We may be performing rather than worshipping, seeking compliments or approval, or indulging in self-pride.

Just as others can't tell if we are truly worshipping, neither can anyone know if the behaviors we exhibit are proper indications of salvation and worship. First Samuel 16:7 reminds us of this: "But the LORD said

---

17. Edwards, *Religious Affections*, 54.
18. Edwards, *Religious Affections*, 63.

to Samuel, 'Do not look on his appearance or on the height of his stature, because I have rejected him. For the LORD sees not as man sees; man looks on the outward appearance, but the LORD looks on the heart.'"

THE IMPORTANCE OF THE SIGNS OF NOTHING

No one can see inside the heart and mind of an individual except God, but we can observe the continual nature of the change that has occurred in a person over time. Paul reminds us in Galatians 5:22–23 that "the fruit of the Spirit is love, joy, peace, patience, kindness, goodness, faithfulness, gentleness, self-control; against such things there is no law" and in Ephesians 5:9 that "the fruit of light is found in all that is good and right and true." Nevertheless, appearances can be deceiving, especially those that appear briefly before disappearing, which is often one of the characteristics of false signs of gracious and holy affections. We need to recognize that not all physical responses in worship are truly spiritual responses. For this reason, our pastors and worship leaders must target a genuine spiritual response in worship. We must focus on growing in ourselves and in our congregations true gracious and holy affections to Christ.

Understanding what we must do, however, is only the beginning. Knowing how to reach our target is essential. How do we do that? How do we help our congregations to seek more than an emotional rush from the music we sing? This is the focus of the following chapters.

8

The Pattern

Oh, magnify the LORD with me, and let us exalt his name together! Psalm 34:3

Are you aware that there are right and wrong ways to worship God? God cares about worship, about how we worship him. We see this throughout scripture, beginning in Genesis: "In the beginning, God created the heavens and the earth" (Gen 1:1). In those words, "we find the very foundation for all biblical religion"[1] and, in essence, the foundation of all biblical worship. Through his creation, God declares his glory: "The heavens declare the glory of God, and the sky above proclaims his handiwork" (Ps 19:1). Through this creation, he establishes "the very basis of and foundation for worship."[2]

One of the joys of living where my wife and I do is the drive home in the evening. Often, we drive right into a beautiful sunset. Each one is unique in its colorful array. We see God's glory in every creative example that he provides. How much more would that have been true for Adam and Eve in the pristine garden with God's presence on display? Inspiration to worship him would have been prolific. As we design worship for our churches, we will do well to keep that worship closely tied to what God has instructed so that we can see his glory on full display.

When it comes to worship, God has very strong opinions. Scripture gives us examples of how worship should and should not be done. Because God cares about how we worship him, we must take great care to honor his

---

1. Aniol, *Changed from Glory into Glory*, 21.
2. Aniol, *Changed from Glory into Glory*, 21.

desires when we lead, plan, or participate in congregational worship experiences. Targeting gracious and holy affections involves all aspects of our worship services, not just the music. First, we will look at what belongs in a worship service and the scriptural foundations for those aspects of worship. Then, in subsequent chapters, we will look specifically at the musical decisions we make as worship leaders to help our congregations grow in gracious and holy affections for Christ.

WORSHIP

The first and second commandments show God's particular care regarding worship (Exod 20:2–6). The Israelites were to have "no other gods" (v. 3) and no "carved image[s]" (v. 4). Isaiah reiterates this sentiment in Isaiah 42:8: "I am the LORD; that is my name; my glory I give to no other, nor my praise to carved idols." God shares the stage with no one. Scripture "demands that only Yahweh be worshiped as the sole divinity or God. All other 'gods' (supernatural beings such as angels) are to be understood and appreciated for their roles in the universe, but only Yahweh is divine."[3]

In Exodus 25, God instructs the Israelites to create a tabernacle: "And let them make me a sanctuary, that I may dwell in their midst" (v. 8). He goes on to give precise directions regarding the building of the tabernacle so that everything is done "after the pattern . . . shown you" (v. 40). In verse 2, God commands Moses to "speak to the people of Israel, that they take for me a contribution." He then proceeds to detail every item that should be included in that offering: special metals, fabrics, skins, woods, oils, spices, and stones. All of these were to be used "exactly as I show you concerning the pattern of the tabernacle, and of all its furniture, so you shall make it" (v. 9). Throughout the book of Exodus, God gives Moses specifics about offerings, feasts, and altars, everything he expected to be part of worshipping him.

FALSE WORSHIP

The Bible also contains negative examples, showing us the kinds of worship unacceptable to God. These examples highlight approaches to worship that are inconsistent with God's desires for his people: the rejection of Cain's

---

3. Stuart, *Exodus*, 449.

offering in Genesis 4, the golden calf incident in Exodus 32, Nadab and Abihu's offering of "strange fire" in Leviticus 10, God's rejection of Saul in 1 Samuel 15, Jesus's rejection of pharisaical worship in Matthew 15, and Ananias and Sapphira's lies and theft in Acts 5.

Cain and Abel

In the first worship war,[4] Cain killed his brother Abel over worship. Scripture tells us that God "had regard for Abel and his offering" but "had no regard" for Cain's offering (Gen 4:4–5). God clearly rejected Cain's offering, but why? Why did God accept Abel's offering and reject Cain's offering? At the outset of study, it is difficult to know. The reason seems to be twofold: his offering was insufficient according to God's requirement, and his heart was not right in making the offering (Gen 4:3–8). Determining with precision which it was is impossible; Genesis does not make the reason clear. However, some scholars have argued that other places in scripture help us clear this up. Hebrews 11:4a states, "By faith Abel offered to God a more acceptable sacrifice than Cain, through which he was commended as righteous." Jude 11 states that Cain abandoned himself "for the sake of gain." First John 3:12 clarifies that Cain's "deeds were evil" while his brother's were "righteous." According to Scott Aniol, "These descriptions relate most specifically to the inward spiritual condition of the men, yet Hebrews also notes that Abel's sacrifice itself was 'more excellent' than Cain's, and this righteousness was determined by 'his gifts.'"[5] Both the gift and how it is given seem to be important to God.

This account challenges us today concerning both our attitude and action in worship. We should worship God not only with the right heart but also with the right sacrifice or elements of worship.

The Golden Calf

The golden calf incident exemplifies how worship cannot be offered merely according to our values and tastes (Exod 32). The people decided they wanted to see their god instead of accepting that he was only spirit and could not be seen. Douglas K. Stuart reminds us that "it was so much easier

---

4. Aniol, *Changed from Glory into Glory*, 23.
5. Aniol, *Changed from Glory into Glory*, 24.

to believe in something that could actually be seen."⁶ In this experience, they pressured Aaron to create for them "gods who shall go before us" (Exod 32:1). The shocking reality of that statement is that they didn't realize that God, Yahweh God, had already gone before them. In addition to desiring visible gods, they wanted to connect the worship of Yahweh with the worship of the culture they had just left behind. On the fly, they designed a worship system that was a "syncretism of Yahwism with the Egyptian bull cult."⁷ This powerful incident is cautionary for those of us attempting to worship an invisible, eternally past, and eternally future God who is Lord of all and should clearly be the one designing our worship experiences. If the Israelites, who had seen the power of God part the waters of the Red Sea, could be tempted to worship God wrongly, we could potentially do the same.

Nadab and Abihu

One Saturday night, when I was eight years old, I was at a youth revival service with my mom. A young lady from the church's youth group was up front sharing her testimony. During that testimony, I got scared and told my mom as much. She said we would talk about it when we got home. When we got home, my dad was home from his second shift job. That night, the three of us knelt in front of the brown plaid couch in our living room, and I declared my faith in Jesus as my Lord and my Savior. That night, a Holy Spirit-derived fear of God led me to salvation. In Leviticus 10, we find the story of Nadab and Abihu, an extraordinary event that should give us pause and foster in us a reverent fear of God.

Nadab and Abihu were Aaron's sons. They had responsibilities related to Israel's worship of Yahweh as "God had consecrated Aaron and his sons to the holy vocation of the priesthood."⁸ They had been instructed by God through Moses: "'At the entrance of the tent of meeting you shall remain day and night for seven days, performing what the LORD has charged, so that you do not die, for so I have been commanded.' And Aaron and his sons did all the things that the LORD commanded by Moses" (Lev 8:35–36). The Bible says, however, that they "each took his censer⁹ and put fire in it and

---

6. Stuart, *Exodus*, 663.
7. Stuart, *Exodus*, 663.
8. Sproul, "Strange Fire," para. 2.
9. Sproul describes a censer as "a kind of vessel that was used in antiquity to contain

laid incense on it and offered unauthorized fire before the LORD which he had not commanded them" (Lev 10:1). Other translations call this fire "strange" (KJV), "unacceptable" (AMP), and "unholy" (RSV). What exactly qualified this fire as being unauthorized we don't know. It could be that they left their post at the "entrance of the tent" and got fire somewhere else. It could be that it wasn't their job to offer the fire. The result of this infraction was God bringing fire upon these sons of Aaron and extinguishing their lives.

This is why it is so essential that the designers of our worship services be well-trained theologians. Creative worship that stays within the bounds of God's instructions in his word is a blessing. Creative worship that goes beyond God's instructions will damage the church. Nadab and Abihu had disobeyed God's commands regarding the proper way to worship him. Clearly, how we worship matters to God. In this story, God determined the infraction was sufficient to snuff out the lives of two young priests.

Would God do the same in our day if we worship him incorrectly? I don't think so. But should this story create in us a holy fear of God that motivates us to worship him according to his desires? I think it should!

Saul's Disobedience to the Lord

First Samuel 15 recounts King Saul's disobeying God regarding the destruction of the Amalekites. God commanded Saul to completely destroy this nation, including their livestock (v. 3); but Saul decided to save the best for himself, claiming that he was keeping the best animals so that he could sacrifice them to God. Samuel was a judge set aside for service to God since his birth. God showed Samuel what Saul had done. When Samuel confronted Saul, he spoke these words:

> Has the LORD as great delight in burnt offerings and sacrifices,
> as in obeying the voice of the LORD?
> Behold, to obey is better than sacrifice,
> and to listen than the fat of rams.
> For rebellion is as the sin of divination,
> and presumption is as iniquity and idolatry.
> Because you have rejected the word of the LORD,
> he has also rejected you from being king. (1 Sam 15:22–23)

---

the incense that was burned as an offering before God." Sproul, "Strange Fire," para. 2.

This chilling declaration from God spoken through Samuel to King Saul shows that God rejected Saul because of his disobedience.

According to Robert D. Bergen, "And Samuel, as God's unyielding spiritual advocate, could not permit God's primary political and military representative to get by with only partial obedience. Partial obedience was in fact disobedience."[10] This reality should cause us to think seriously about how we worship. The leadership of our churches should spend time in the word, in prayer, and in study and preparation, seeking God regarding what we should or should not do in a gathering for worship. God cares and we should honor him in our congregational gatherings.

Jesus's Confrontation of Tradition

One day, the Pharisees came to Jesus to complain: "'Why do your disciples break the tradition of the elders? For they do not wash their hands when they eat?'" (Matt 15:2). Jesus turned their words back on them, calling them hypocrites because of the way they twisted the law to their advantage. In rebuking them, Jesus quoted Isaiah:

> "This people honors me with their lips,
> but their heart is far from me;
> in vain do they worship me,
> teaching as doctrines the commandments of men." (Matt 15:8–9)

This incident is another prime example of God showing his desire for biblical worship.

In our worship, are we following the teachings of scripture or the doctrines and commandments of men? If we worship God with our traditions, whether they be five-hundred-year-old traditions, fifty-year-old traditions, or five-minute-old traditions and our hearts are far from God, then we waste our time in worship. We must follow the word of God in our worship *and* honor him with our heart's affections if we hope to truly worship him the way he desires to be worshipped.

Ananias and Sapphira's Lying and Stealing

Ananias and Sapphira sold a piece of land and committed the proceeds to God. However, "with his wife's knowledge he kept back for himself some of

---

10. Bergen, *1, 2 Samuel*, 172.

the proceeds and brought only a part of it and laid it at the apostles' feet" (Acts 5:2). The word used for "hold back" is *nosphizo*, which carries the meaning of stealing, pilfering, or embezzling.[11] These definitions help us to understand that this couple had indeed committed all of the proceeds to the church but then had stolen them back. You cannot embezzle what is already yours, only that which belongs to someone else. Giving to God is an act of worship; and clearly, in this instance, Ananias and Saphira were hypocritical in how they worshipped God.

This incident should cause us to deeply consider the instructions of God as we design and participate in the worship of the Triune God. How the church worships God should be holy worship. Not only should we gather with hearts filled with the Holy Spirit, but we should also do what scripture instructs in our worship gatherings. Proper worship is worship that includes following godly instructions from his word done with the right heart by the worshipper.

These examples show there are, indeed, right ways and wrong ways to worship God. As they show, God cares profoundly about how we worship him. So how do we ensure acceptable worship? The 1689 Baptist Confession of Faith states,

> The acceptable way of worshiping the true God, is instituted by himself, and so limited by his own revealed will, that he may not be worshiped according to the imagination and devices of men, nor the suggestions of Satan, under any visible representations, or any other way not prescribed in the Holy scriptures.[12]

Throughout scripture, God has shown us how to worship him; we would be wise to follow his teachings.

In full disclosure, I haven't always agreed with this sentiment. I felt that the way we worshipped was up to us. I often quoted 2 Corinthians 3:17: "Now the Lord is the Spirit, and where the Spirit of the Lord is, there is freedom." Of course, in context, this verse refers to the freedom we find in Christ and the veil over our hearts being removed. We should remember

---

11. Polhill states, "The verb means to pilfer, to purloin, to embezzle. One does not embezzle one's own funds but those of another, in this instance those that rightfully belonged to the common Christian fund. Significantly, the same rare verb occurs in the Greek version of Josh 7:1–26, the story of Achan, who took from Jericho some of the booty 'devoted' (i.e., set aside for God) for sacred use." Polhill, *Acts*, 156.

12. "Of Religious Worship and the Sabbath Day," *The 1689 Baptist Confession of Faith*, para. 1.

that God has allowed much freedom in worship. He hasn't prescribed the order or the songs, what texts to read or preach, how long the service should last, and so forth. However, he has prescribed some things, and we would do well to follow his instructions.

These examples of false worship in the Bible are scary to me. They highlight God's deep concern for how men worship him. As I read the Old Testament, it appears God is most displeased with his people when they worship him incorrectly. This is why I feel so strongly about following the regulative principle when it comes to congregational worship. We should worship God as he desires, not only according to what he does not prohibit. I seriously doubt if Nadab and Abihu knew they were going to die that day. I do believe they knew that they were going rogue in worship. They probably knew that they were breaking the rules that God had established. God did not accept their creativity in worship. I would suggest that we should allow God to be the designer of our worship and let the word of God interpret what that means in our churches.

TRUE WORSHIP

Throughout scripture, numerous instances of genuine worship guide us on how we should worship God. I have selected a few prime examples for us to consider. This sampling represents a diverse group of different types of worship: Adam and Eve in the garden in Genesis 2, worship before the Ark (Davidic worship) in 1 Chronicles 15 and 16, the commissioning of Isaiah in Isaiah 6, the fellowship of believers in Acts 2, and a glimpse of heaven in Revelation 4 and 5.

Adam and Eve in the Garden

Before sin in the garden, Adam and Eve lived an existence that none of us will ever experience on this side of heaven. They were allowed to worship God and relate to one another without barriers or the restrictions of sin: "Therefore a man shall leave his father and his mother and hold fast to his wife, and they shall become one flesh. And the man and his wife were both naked and were not ashamed" (Gen 2:24–25). I don't know what the difference would be in worshipping God without shame, but I look forward to the day when our bodies will be glorified and we will see Jesus face to face. First Corinthians 13:12 explains, "For now we see in a mirror dimly, but then face to face. Now I know in part; then I shall know fully, even as I have been fully known." This future hope will somehow restore us to the idyllic experience of the garden. For us now, our worship is burdened by our existence in these cursed bodies. Romans 8:22–23 declares, "For we know that the whole creation has been groaning together in the pains of childbirth until now. And not only the creation, but we ourselves, who have the firstfruits of the Spirit, groan inwardly as we wait eagerly for adoption as sons, the redemption of our bodies."

Adam and Eve give us the slightest glimpse of what we may anticipate. We have the hope that one day we will worship Jesus face to face. Each time we gather as believers, we get another obscure taste of what heavenly worship will be like. While that taste is oh so sweet, the joy we know when we gather is nothing compared to what we will experience one day.

Worship before the Ark (Davidic Worship)

David could have done better in his first attempt to bring the ark into Jerusalem. He did not consult God or his word about the proper way to move the ark, and the result was that Uzzah reached out to stabilize the ark and lost his life in the process (2 Sam 6:5–7). David had the ark taken to Obed-edom's house:

> So, David was not willing to take the ark of the Lord into the city of David. But David took it aside to the house of Obed-edom the Gittite. And the ark of the Lord remained in the house of Obed-edom the Gittite three months, and the Lord blessed Obed-edom and all his household. (2 Sam 6:10–11)

When David realized the blessing that would come from having the ark in Jerusalem, he determined that moving it was worth another attempt; but this time, he consulted the Torah and moved the ark correctly.

We have much to learn from David's experience. The most obvious is that we should do things God's way, according to the instructions of his word. Secondly, when we don't do things God's way, we miss many blessings. How many times have we disregarded God's word and ended up missing out on the blessings that he has for us? This, however, is not the point I'm trying to make. I want us to look at the positive example King David set for us when he designed the worship that occurred before the ark.

The Pattern

Music ministry is firmly established in 1 Chronicles 15 and 16. Instrumentalists, including those who played the harps, lyres, cymbals, bronze cymbals, trumpets, and horns, are all listed (1 Chron 15:16–24). Singers were also added to the praise band (1 Chron 15:16; 16:7). And it must be noted that the music was to be loud! First Chronicles 15:16 states, "David also commanded the chiefs of the Levites to appoint their brothers as the singers who should play loudly on musical instruments, on harps and lyres and cymbals, to raise sounds of joy." And 1 Chronicles 15:28 says again, "So all Israel brought up the ark of the covenant of the Lord with shouting, to the sound of the horn, trumpets, and cymbals, and made loud music on harps and lyres." In my church, we have a lot of instrumentalists on stage, and I have never found a way to avoid making loud music with an orchestra full of brass instruments, drums, cymbals, pianos, and so forth. Musical instruments get loud, and it seems that is how the Lord likes them!

Leadership was also recruited for the worship in this example. Chenaniah was the overall leader: "Chenaniah, leader of the Levites in music, should direct the music, for he understood it" (1 Chron 15:22). In verse 27, we see a little more detail: "Chenaniah the leader of the music of the singers." Chenaniah directed the music and, apparently, the singers as well.

The phrase "for he understood it" is significant. We need leaders who understand the church's worship for it to reach its full potential. That understanding involves much. Our music and worship leadership must understand leadership, music, theology, discipleship, and church culture. The mission statement for the worship ministries division at Midwestern Baptist Theological Seminary states, "We exist to prepare musician-theologians for the Church who will faithfully serve, build, strengthen, or lead her corporate worship among her generations no matter her cultural song."[13] Somewhere along the way, many churches have decided that this level of understanding is no longer necessary. If a leader can play a guitar or keyboard and sing well, he or she is qualified to lead the church's worship.

Please understand that I have great compassion for those churches that struggle to have even one person leading their worship. My mom was in a church that used videos to lead their worship. She was so excited when the church found a young man with a guitar to lead their worship. That is often the case, and we should celebrate those leaders.

I know of another church that, several years ago, had its worship leadership retire. The church's response was to promote the student worship

---

13. Midwestern Baptist Theological Seminary, opening statement.

leader to the main worship leader position. When this new leader said he was incapable of leading the church's choir and orchestra, the church disbanded those ministries. To this day, the church does not have a choir or orchestra.

We need trained leadership guiding the music and worship ministries in the church for many reasons. I am not saying that every church should have a choir and orchestra. However, I love those ministries for their effectiveness and ability to involve many church and community members in ministry. I am saying church decisions should be based on strategic planning in worship. When leadership is lacking, perhaps the church could provide the training and help to grow and improve the worship of the church. An individual staff member's skill level should not determine the church's worship ministry. The word of God should be the determining factor.

My brother often joins our orchestra for special events. He likes to call the worship at CBC temple worship. What he means is that we utilize many of the instruments described in Davidic worship in our services. I'm not suggesting that anyone model their worship based on CBC's approach, but we should base our worship on biblical examples. This model may currently be beyond the scope of possibility for your church. Even so, I would encourage you to raise the bar as high as possible as you recruit and train musicians for worship leadership in your setting.[14]

The Commissioning of Isaiah

In Isaiah 6:1–3, scripture records an extraordinary moment of worship that changed Isaiah moving forward:[15]

> In the year that King Uzziah died I saw the Lord sitting upon a throne, high and lifted up; and the train of his robe filled the temple. Above him stood the seraphim. Each had six wings: with two he covered his face, and with two he covered his feet, and with two he flew. And one called to another and said: "Holy, holy, holy is the Lord of hosts; the whole earth is full of his glory!"

Isaiah was granted a vision that none of us will likely experience this side of heaven. I don't include this to presume that we should hope for

---

14. See chapter 11 for worship leaders for more help in this area.

15. According to Smith, "The experience of having a glimpse of the majesty of God's glory dramatically impacted his theology and caused him to understand God's purpose for his life in a new way." Smith, *Isaiah 1–39*, 183.

this kind of experience in our churches but to point out what we can glean from his experience. We can learn from this experience a way to shape our worship. Bruce Leafblad suggests that we can order our worship gatherings according to Isaiah's experience:

- Divine revelation ("I saw the Lord." v. 1)
- Adoration ("Holy, holy, holy is the Lord of hosts; the whole earth is full of his glory!" v. 3)
- Confession ("Woe is me! For I am lost; for I am a man of unclean lips, and I dwell in the midst of a people of unclean lips." v. 5)
- Expiation ("Behold, this [burning coal] has touched your lips; your guilt is taken away, and your sin atoned for." v. 7)
- Proclamation ("Whom shall I send and who will go for us?" v. 8)
- Dedication ("Here I am! Send me." v. 8)
- Supplication ("How long, O Lord?" v. 11)
- Commission ("Until the cities lie waste without inhabitant." v. 11) [16]

We can design congregational worship services with this format in mind. Even if a church doesn't attempt to utilize this model for every service, this order is an excellent way to design a special night of worship.

The Fellowship of Believers in Acts 2

The New Testament references various churches that Paul, the other apostles, and New Testament authors and evangelists wrote and ministered to. No story in the New Testament is more fundamental to the burgeoning church than the second chapter of Acts: "And day by day, attending the temple together and breaking bread in their homes, they received their food with glad and generous hearts, praising God and having favor with all the people. And the Lord added to their number day by day those who were being saved" (vv. 46–47).

According to John B. Polhill, this description of the New Testament church's communal life and worship "could almost be described as the young church's 'age of innocence' . . . present[ing] an ideal for the Christian community which it must always strive for, constantly return to, and

---

16. Aniol, "Biblical Foundations."

discover anew if it is to have that unity of spirit and purpose essential for an effective witness."[17] Likewise, Curtis Vaughn shares, "The Christian fellowship was marked by worship and joy," and that "three expressions characterize[d] the disciples' worship: 'daily,'... 'with one accord,' ... and 'in the temple.'"[18] This communal aspect of the church has waned as our culture has grown more separated with our automatic garage doors and privacy fences. We have lost the sense of true community.

Every church I know is working to restore believers' sense of belonging through discipleship and fellowship ministries. How do we accomplish this in congregational worship? We gather in the church building to worship in one accord, believe we are family, and show our commitment to each other. Gathering in the church building has profound value and is biblically supported. If meeting together was good enough for the first-century Christians, it should be good enough for us.

A Glimpse of Heaven in Revelation

The revelation of Jesus Christ offers many extravagant scenes of worship. I've been involved in and led worship many times. I have seen the power of God at work in the lives of believers and begin a new work in those just being saved. I've seen twelve nations come together in worship while being led by a praise team from four nations. I've heard language upon language that gave voice to the word of God. God has done extraordinary things in worship. But I have never seen twenty-four thrones with twenty-four elders (Rev 4). I've never seen the Lion of the tribe of Judah open the scrolls (Rev 5). I've never seen angelic beings in flight. I've never seen a multitude that could not be numbered (Rev 7). (Trust me, we count all of them every Sunday!) I've never seen many of the things and beings that the Spirit inspired John to describe.

What I have seen is that same Jesus, the one they declared, "Worthy are you, our Lord and God, to receive glory and honor and power, for you created all things, and by your will they existed and were created" (Rev 4:11). I have seen believers declare "to him who sits on the throne and to the Lamb be blessing and honor and glory and might forever and ever!" (Rev 5:13). I look with great hope to the day when I see this:

---

17. Polhill, *Acts*, 122.
18. Vaughan, *Acts*, 33.

The Pattern

> After this I looked, and behold, a great multitude that no one could number, from every nation, from all tribes and peoples and languages, standing before the throne and before the Lamb, clothed in white robes, with palm branches in their hands, and crying out with a loud voice, "Salvation belongs to our God who sits on the throne, and to the Lamb!" (Rev 7:9–10).

I have also looked with much expectancy to see what John saw: "Then I saw a new heaven and a new earth, for the first heaven and the first earth had passed away, and the sea was no more" (Rev 21:1).

I love to worship. I love leading my church in worship. But I cannot wait until I worship in heaven. I look with great anticipation to the day when I will see him face to face and worship with the throng, unencumbered with the load of sin that our worshippers struggle with now. With the heart of the beloved, I say, "He who testifies to these things says, 'Surely I am coming soon.' Amen. Come, Lord Jesus!" (Rev 22:20).

WORSHIP AND DISCIPLESHIP

Worship equals discipleship. Everything we do in a worship service disciples the people to understand what we value as a church and what God values. If we pump up the crowd to get them excited, they will learn to believe that excitement is what's important and that is what they will expect each week. If we read scripture in worship, they will value it and begin expecting it each week. If we spend time praying, they will understand that prayer is essential. Because what we do disciples our congregations, everything we do in a service should be worship. This leads us back to the definition of worship we started with in chapter 1: Worship is intentionally setting one's heart and affection on Christ in order to declare His worth.

As worship leaders of New Testament churches, we follow one of two principles in deciding what to include in our worship services: regulative or normative. As we stated in chapter 1, if we follow the regulative principle, we only include those elements specified in scripture in our worship services. If we follow the normative principle, we may include anything not explicitly forbidden in scripture. At CBC, we follow the regulative principle because of our deep respect for God and his word. For me, reading through the stories in the previous section, False Worship, gives me pause. Those examples and others have caused me to realize that God deeply cares about how we worship him. His anger is most exposed when his people fail

The Worship Target

to worship him correctly. As the designer of our worship moments, I feel responsible for the integrity of the target of our worship. Therefore, to the best of my ability, we only include those elements that God has prescribed for congregational worship.

Following the regulative principle, our worship services consist of seven elements specified in scripture:

- Reading the word (1 Tim 4:13)
- Preaching the word (2 Tim 4:2)
- Singing the word (Col 3; Eph 5)
- Praying the word (1 Tim 2:1)
- Seeing the word through the ordinances: baptism (Matt 28:16–20) and the partaking of the Lord's table (1 Cor 11)
- Giving (1 Cor 16:2)

Our typical order of service follows this pattern: preservice and worship service. The preservice is the time set aside for announcements via slides and the Loop (video announcements). The worship service includes these elements:

- Scripture reading and prayer led by the deacon of the week
- Baptism (generally once a month)
- Music (generally four songs interspersed with scripture readings)
- Prayer by the worship pastor
- Preaching
- Invitation
- The Lord's Supper (when it is observed)

Not every service may contain all seven elements, but most do.

If I could get away from making announcements, I would; but the reality is that they are here to stay. So, at CBC, we do our best to get the information across with as little impact on worship as possible. Our announcements are placed on slides or in a video called The Loop during the time allotted to announcements. The service hasn't formally begun yet, as people are still coming into the worship center and the worship team is getting in place. If we have a significant announcement that needs a personal touch, we will share that after the video loop or at the end of the service after the invitation. Our worship officially begins with the reading of the scripture of the day and it ends with the invitation. Therefore, the announcements are outside our time of worship.

Reading scripture has evolved in the seven years I've been at CBC. I used to read just a verse or few that related to the music we were singing. But I've been convicted that that is not enough. Now, I read entire psalms in context, not just the parts that pertain to the music. We've also begun having one deacon each week read the scripture of the week and offer prayer at the beginning of the worship service. These men are usually a bit uncomfortable doing this, yet they do so, discipling all of us humbly. I also often read scriptures between our songs, showing the theological connection between scripture and that morning's music.

The music usually consists of three to five songs, three or four with the congregation standing and the last with them seated. The final song is often more of a choir special, but the congregation is always invited to sing along (and they do!). After that final piece, I offer prayer, bridging between the music we've just sung and the preaching to come. After the senior pastor presents the word through preaching, we have an invitation. Although we don't have many come forward during the invitation,[19] this serves as a time of reflection, praise, and preparation for the Lord's Supper, which is the last element in our services when it is observed.

By this point, you should understand what should be included in a worship service. I hope you know that God cares about what we do in worship and how we do it. Scripture is full of worship experiences; the ones in this chapter are just a few.

But what about the music? How do we choose the right music to target worship with gracious and holy affections for Christ? The answers are in two parts. First, we will look at the music itself. We will answer how we create beautiful music that our congregations are capable of singing. Then, we will deal with the theology of the music. We will answer what the Bible says about what we should sing. Together, we have the criteria to ensure the music we sing and play targets holy and gracious affections for Christ.

---

19. Most of our new members come from our Welcome to Concord class, which also presents the plan of salvation.

9

Music: Beautiful and Singable

> Then Moses and the people of Israel sang this song to the LORD, saying, "I will sing to the LORD, for he has triumphed gloriously." EXODUS 15:1

EVERY ELEMENT OF A worship service is important, all working together to focus us on worshipping with gracious and holy affections. Worship leaders are primarily responsible for selecting, preparing, and presenting the music during our worship services. When I conducted a conference recently, I offered the group three options for the title: (1) "Planning Worship," (2) "Pickin' Hymns," or (3) "How to Select Theologically Rich Hymnody for Church Revitalization." The first is certainly simple and to the point. The second is what happens all too often. It's simple: pick four songs a week ahead and put them in the Planning Center and ProPresenter. Pickin' hymns equals planning worship. Sometimes, however, we get busy or are not as organized as we should be and are choosing hymns just before services begin. I remember once having my wife drive the thirty minutes to church so I could pick the hymns for that week's service on the way. I could get by with that because I didn't have to worry about getting the words to the tech guys so they could project them on the screen. We had no projection capabilities. The congregation used hymn books. When we finally started introducing new scripture choruses, we put booklets in each pew alongside the hymnals.

The third option, "How to Select Theologically Rich Hymnody for Church Revitalization," seems highly formal, even laughable. Yet that's really what we are talking about here. The terms *hymnody* and *church*

Music: Beautiful and Singable

revitalization may seem unrelatable. Why worry about hymnody? A hymn's a hymn. And what does music have to do with church revitalization? By the end of this chapter, we will see the connections.

As we choose how to implement each element in our services, especially the music portion, we must remember the worship target: worshipping with gracious and holy affections for Christ. Gracious and holy affections are housed in the upper soul, combining the head and heart. Therefore, our songs should reflect the mindful intentionality of deeply theological lyrics that reveal the vibrant reality of love for the Savior. The text, key, tempo, and arrangement of a song all inform our decisions. Two arrangements of the same song can target and elicit vastly different emotions from the congregation.

I rely on three criteria to select the music for any given worship service. The goal is for the songs to be (1) musically beautiful, (2) congregationally singable, and (3) theologically deep. In full disclosure, I stole these criteria from Keith Getty. At a Getty Sing! Conference I attended, he stated that they wanted to sing musically beautiful, congregationally singable, and theologically deep songs. That was the most important thing I took away from that conference, and I began teaching those concepts to my worship team. Let's look at some objective criteria to help churches make beautiful music.

MUSICALLY BEAUTIFUL

One day, our ten-month-old granddaughter stood up at the ottoman and started dancing to the oldies rock music we had been playing. She had yet to learn what the song was about, as a matter of fact she had yet to learn how to walk! She just loved the beat and was responding to the music. Everyone in your congregation is the same way. I enjoy watching that video occasionally; today, when I watched it again, I was reminded of two things. First, my granddaughter is adorable! Second, she reminded me of just how hard it is for worship leaders to convey the most essential message of the universe, the gospel of Jesus Christ, all while distracting the people with beautiful music. What a conundrum! We do our best to make the music beautiful, theologically profound, and engaging while the people are just grooving to the music!

Does that mean we shouldn't try to make the music beautiful? No, of course not. We should attempt tremendous and beautiful music, but we must also be aware that the music may distract the congregation from the message. The fundamental challenge for us, as both worshippers and worship leaders, is how to get the message of our songs heard or properly sung when the music is so powerful. The opposing problem is also challenging. Bad music is much more distracting than beautiful music.

The music selection process is challenging at best and often terribly tricky. To ensure that the music I choose is musically beautiful, I consider these four requirements: (1) attainability, (2) culture, (3) preparation, and (4) quality. Each must be carefully considered when finalizing the music for any service.

Attainability

First, we need to choose music that our worship teams can attain so that they can actually perform skillfully and competently. It's better to be good than complex! The musicians that make up the worship ministry at any church usually encompass a variety of skill levels. They may have been playing or singing for years, have studied and honed their craft, and can tackle anything we throw at them. Or they may be relatively new at their craft, with little or no formal training, and struggle to play basic C, G, and D chords or sight read the simplest of music. We must know our teams to ensure our selected music is within their capabilities. This is especially true when we have a mix of highly skilled musicians and novices. That's one of the beautiful realities of church music that produces wonderful discipleship between musicians.

One season in our church, we were blessed with four guitar players: one acoustic player and one electric who were both seasoned pros and one electric and one acoustic player who were high school students. I scheduled one pro with one high school student each week. That way, we had a good, strong player each week and provided discipleship for the younger players. I'm happy to report that they are all still actively playing in church music ministries. Knowing our musicians is vital to selecting music our groups can play and sing successfully and to growing our musicians.

Culture

Second, we have to know the culture of the churches in which we serve. What will work well in the context of that culture? A church member once told me we hadn't sung his favorite song in a long time. He was right; I had neglected to sing that song for a while. It wasn't one of my favorites, but it was his. So, I ensured that that song made it into a service in the very near future. I'm not suggesting that we plan worship by popular vote, but we do need to acknowledge the likes and dislikes of our congregations to some extent. Music speaks to people; sometimes, they need to know that we also hear them.

Culture is also important when we are trying to expand our worship ministry's musical creativity and our congregation's acceptance of styles that may not be their favorites. I teach a music appreciation class in a high-security prison. At the start of the latest semester, I told the class what kind of music I listen to. I also asked them about their music experiences and what they liked. The class revealed a lot of diversity in musical styles, including classical, country, rock, gospel, and hip-hop. Replicating the music of our culture in congregational worship may sound like a good idea. But, in all honesty, that is nearly impossible. I told the guys in my class I would listen to some of their music if they offered good suggestions (and I did). However, that didn't mean that we were going to study their music in class. Just because a congregation loves a specific type of music doesn't mean that that style must show up on Sunday morning.

As we lead our churches toward worshipping with gracious and holy affections, we may be introducing different songs and arrangements that are not in their wheelhouse, so to speak. We need to be aware of this and realize we must lead gently. Leadership is a fine thread. Pull too hard or make too many changes too fast, and the thread may break. So be aware of the church culture, including that of the worship team, and don't leave the congregation or members of the worship team behind.

Preparation

We must be well prepared. The best way to make beautiful music is to ensure our worship teams are adequately prepared. What that entails may vary from church to church, so I can't fully answer the question for every group. I can answer it for mine. I have our team rehearse until we get it right. My group usually requires a two-hour Wednesday evening rehearsal each week and a brief sound check and warm-up on Sunday morning. We don't move on to the next song in rehearsal until the one we are working on can be played and sung well without needing to stop. Sometimes, we need to add rehearsals for various sections. Other times, we add one-on-one work with individual musicians. The point is that to play and sing beautiful music, a church music and worship ministry must do what it takes to get it right.

My son plays guitar on the praise team for his church. They generally rehearse on Thursday evenings. If I call him earlier in the week, he commonly tells me he is practicing for rehearsal. I love that! Church musicians must practice for the upcoming rehearsal to contribute without slowing down the rehearsal process. When the entire team does that, we have the time to worship with the song (in rehearsal) and not just focus on the music. Encourage your team to practice alone so they can enjoy rehearsing together. One of our praise team singers consistently knows the songs better than me by the time we get to the Wednesday rehearsal. She is always ready to go and willing to lead the song if needed. Remember, our goal is to ensure the music aids in worshipping Jesus rather than distracting from him.

Quality

The ultimate requirement is quality. Quality trumps style every time. We have heard lots of music in our lifetimes. I can listen to almost any style of music and enjoy it if it is done well. (In fact, since my class's suggestions, I've listened to some hip-hop recently!) Church worship ministries need to understand this concept. One Sunday morning, I attended a church that had a "blended" worship service. They sang hymns and "not too" contemporary songs. As I sat in the back worshipping with them, I noticed their pianist was very good at playing the hymns, but she couldn't play a syncopation to save her life. Almost all contemporary music has some level of syncopation, so if you can't play syncopations, you can't play contemporary worship music properly. I wasn't their consultant that day, but had I been I would have suggested they only sing hymns. Not only would doing so make the music more beautiful, but it also would give them a unique voice in their community.

That said, I am not suggesting churches choose a particular style to draw people in. But if they do, the worship leader needs to ensure the music is handled excellently. Poor quality will only lead to poor outcomes.

Sometimes, attaining the quality we want means learning new things and finding new ways to do the same things. We have an alto on our praise team that I asked to sing a song that was a good bit out of her comfortable singing range. Instead of rejecting the suggestion, she went online and took voice lessons to increase her range. Not only can she sing that particular song, but she can now sing other songs that are rangy for her. That is a beautiful picture of making sacrifices to improve the quality of our music in worship.

CONGREGATIONALLY SINGABLE

The primary ensemble in every church is the congregation. Every church would be blessed if those who plan and lead congregational worship kept that truth in mind. Every member of every church needs to worship God. The rallying cry of church worship ministries should be Psalm 34:3: "Oh, magnify the LORD with me, and let us exalt his name together!" We often forget the "together" part. Whether the church is a choir and orchestra church or a rock band church, the congregation can be left in the dust of grand anthems or smoke-filled, laser-lit worship shows, wondering how they fit in. Am I a spectator or a worshipper?

What should we consider, then, as we plan worship for the modern church? How can we engage the congregation in present-day worship? We need to consider these elements to determine whether a piece of music is congregationally singable: (1) key, (2) vocal range, (3) rhythm, and (4) technology.

Key

We need to choose keys that the average church member can sing in. Few of us can sing in the keys many popular Christian artists use in their music. We should choose music in the keys that our congregations can sing comfortably, or they won't sing.

I am blessed in that I am a baritone. I haven't always considered that a blessing. I have often wished that I was a high tenor. Why do I now see being a baritone as a blessing? Most of the men in my congregation are not high tenors either, and being a baritone has forced me to choose keys that most guys can sing. I followed a fantastic tenor at my church. In one of the first rehearsals I led, the guitarist said, "We've never played this song in this key." I suggested he get used to it. Almost all the keys changed. Being a baritone has forced me to follow a principle that all of us should embrace as we plan worship for our churches: choose keys that the church can sing.

Most modern music is available in a range of keys from publishing websites. With the advent of digital music, we can choose the keys we use when we buy music. No longer are we bound by the hymnal and whatever keys the editorial board has selected for the songs in the hymnal. (The website praisecharts.com has a cool tool where you can choose your vocal range, and it will tell you which key to select for that song to stay in that vocal range.) Knowing that choice is available, we need to choose the keys for both our congregations and our worship teams wisely.

Vocal Range

Vocal ranges are closely related to keys. We need everyone to sing, especially men. At one church where I served, I observed two similar families. Both consisted of the dad, the mom, and two boys. One dad was a union pipe fitter; the other was a union carpenter. The boys were about the same age. The families even lived on the same road. One massive difference between them was that one dad sang on Sunday mornings; the other did not. The boys were also different. The ones from one family sang; those from the other did not. Which boys sang? The ones whose dad sang. I've observed that if men don't sing during worship, their sons won't either. But the reverse is also true: when men sing, their sons are likely to sing as well. The dads in our congregations need to sing and to disciple their sons to sing. As worship leaders, we need to choose songs that men are comfortable singing.

Choosing songs with singable vocal ranges is the key to a singing congregation. What are suitable vocal ranges for your church? Bob Kauflin says, "My basic approach is to keep songs from a low A to a high D."[1] If you were to hold to that rule, you would sing "10,000 Reasons" in the key of Eb. We actually sing that song in F. So, we go a step above the rule in our church for that song, which means we ask our congregation to sing a high E. They don't seem to have a problem with that. A congregation can also be asked to sing a song too low. There is a sweet spot for your congregation. I would encourage you to find it.[2]

We must be concerned not only with the song's vocal range but also the tessitura, which is how long the song stays in a particular range. Most men

---

1. Kauflin, "Finding the Right Key," para. 1.
2. "Top-10 Loudest NFL Stadiums," para. 46. By the way, at Arrowhead Stadium, the Kansas City Chiefs fans regularly do a singing chant that has every fan singing a high F; and Arrowhead Stadium holds the volume record at 142 decibels.

can endure a quick high note, but continually singing high notes fatigues even a well-trained voice. The previously mentioned "10,000 Reasons" has the high E for one quarter note in the chorus. That one note equals only one beat. It is brief and doesn't occur very often in the song. That's why the song works in the key of F. If we want our men to sing, we have to consider their vocal abilities. The men who spend their weeks working behind a desk, on construction sites, or wherever their work takes them need a place to sing praise to God with the church. When we remember these men in selecting the music for our worship services, we disciple their sons and bless the congregation as a whole.

Why am I targeting this discussion to men? Simply put, for some reason, women are far more likely to sing than men. This presents a significant challenge to those of us designing our worship ministries. However, in a recent conversation with a soprano at our church, she pointed out that she was having vocal issues, saying, "It may be my age affecting my voice." I know this to be true for my ninety-five-year-old mom, who loves to sing but can't belt it out like she did as a younger woman. Therefore, the challenge is not limited to planning songs for men. We also need to consider all those in our congregations who are aging.

The bottom line is that many professional worship leaders who sell out stadiums every night have extraordinary tenor voices. Their example of singing ridiculously high songs filters down to the church. However, those artists should not be the guiding light for church worship ministries. We harm the church by singing songs our people cannot sing. Our job is not to replicate the latest and greatest in contemporary Christian music but to lead our churches to a genuine worship experience that allows them to grow in their gracious and holy affections for Christ.

Rhythm

Complex modern syncopations can be tricky for the average congregation to sing. Syncopation is "a deliberate upsetting of the normal pattern of accents. Instead of falling on the strong beat of the measure, the accent is shifted to a weak beat or offbeat."[3] Young congregations have grown up listening to syncopated rhythms and can handle them more quickly than older congregations. But even those with a few years under their belt can handle modern rhythms if they are actively involved in the worship ministry.

3. Forney et al., *The Enjoyment of Music*, 11.

We cannot entirely avoid syncopated rhythms when singing contemporary music in our worship services. But we must ensure that our congregations can sing the rhythms we are leading. This goes back to the requirement to lead gently. Syncopation is a skill that is not easily mastered. We may need to disciple our musicians to enable them to play such rhythms. For example, with novice musicians, especially drummers, consider starting with simple four-on-the-floor time signatures. I've found that any deviation from that confuses young drummers. Then, by discipling them to add to their skill level until they can handle more complicated rhythms and time signatures, we avoid overwhelming them and unwittingly lowering the quality of the music we present in our worship services. Remember, it's better to be good than complex. Congregations unused to singing syncopated rhythms will appreciate a gentle leadership approach.

I enjoy music with syncopated rhythms. I also enjoy watching the congregation sway back and forth when we sing songs in 6/8 time. For full disclosure, I enjoy teaching my team complicated music with multiple rhythms, time signatures, and dramatic key changes. But I'm most interested in ensuring the congregation is singing with me and worshipping with gracious and holy affections. That is less attainable when they are trying to figure out what to sing or are dropping out of the music portion of the service altogether. By selecting music our congregations and worship teams can understand, sing, and play, we encourage them to participate fully in worship.

Technology

The fourth consideration is the effect the technology we have available may have on congregational worship. The capabilities we now have can overwhelm the message of the music and distract from worship if we don't use them wisely. Volume and lighting are two elements of technology that need to be addressed in many churches. Volume should be immersive but not overwhelming. Too soft is too soft, and too loud is too loud. The average worshipper may feel too inhibited to sing if the music is too soft. Music that is too loud can distract from the purpose of the service. Finding a good, comfortable balance can take some time and practice. However, we should keep in mind what scripture tells us: "So all Israel brought up the ark of the covenant of the LORD with shouting, to the sound of the horn, trumpets, and cymbals, and made loud music on harps and lyres" (1 Chron 15:28).

Music: Beautiful and Singable

So, making loud music is biblical![4] And no matter how hard we try, we will always play and sing either too loudly or softly for some people.

Lights should be up on the congregation. Remember, Paul challenged us to sing to one another.[5] When we keep the worship center relatively dark, with lights shining only on the stage, we isolate the congregation from the worship team and from each other. Some may argue that the lights need to be down on the congregation to avoid distractions from the other worshippers. I agree with that sentiment if you are at a concert. When I attend a concert, I am there to hear the musicians and focus on them; but in worship, I am worshipping with my brothers and sisters in Christ. They are my family; therefore, they cannot be a distraction to my worship because they are part of it. If worship leaders aren't careful, instead of leading in worship, they can quickly become the performance the congregation watches. How can we teach and admonish one another through psalms, hymns, and spiritual songs if we can't see or hear one another? We must treat them as a family of worshippers and the primary ensemble in our churches. In all honesty, I don't have an agenda for lighting, but I use this as one example of how the word of God should help guide us in every area of our congregational worship experiences, even in the technology we use.

Finally, even though I've separated them in this chapter for the purposes of discussion, this criterion of being singable relates directly to the criterion of being musically beautiful, specifically the requirement of attainability. We need to ensure that our singers and instrumentalists who lead congregational worship can handle the music we select. One way to do this is to choose simple music they can sing and play easily. But simple can soon become boring, which also becomes a distraction to worship. And so, while we may start with simple music, we ought to prepare and disciple our teams gradually and adequately to sing and play more challenging music. While we prepare our teams, we are also preparing our congregations to accept different types of music, again leading gently.

And, yes, it's okay to modify things a bit so the music is attainable for our teams and congregations. We need to accept that the rhythms, keys, and vocal ranges of professionals are not always attainable by our worship teams. But, if a particular song is vital to the worship ministry, we can

---

4. If your church has a large instrumental group, like ours, it is nearly impossible to keep the music soft. Brass instruments are loud. However, I have found reminding our players that the lyrics are essential to what we are trying to accomplish helps them to hold back when necessary.

5. See Ephesians 5:19.

certainly make accommodations to present it in a way that is attainable for our teams and congregations and musicians. Remember, the music we present is to lead us to worship Christ with gracious and holy affections, not to prove we can match the skills of professional performing artists. And that leads us to the last of the three criteria: theologically deep.

10

Theologically Deep

> Let the word of Christ dwell in you richly, teaching and admonishing one another in all wisdom, singing psalms and hymns and spiritual songs, with thankfulness in your hearts to God. COLOSSIANS 3:16

I CAME HOME FROM the Getty Sing! Conference in 2018 telling my church that we were going to start setting a goal of singing songs that were musically beautiful, congregationally singable, and theologically deep. Then, one day, when I was teaching a discipleship class[1] on this topic, one of my choir members asked, "Brad, you always say that we should sing songs that are theologically deep, but what exactly does that mean?" I thought the phrase was self-explanatory; but honestly, I couldn't answer his question. Here we are going to do a deep dive to explain what it means to sing theologically deep songs.

Paul reiterates Colossians 3:16 very closely in Ephesians, stating, "addressing one another in psalms and hymns and spiritual songs, singing and making melody to the Lord with your heart" (Eph 5:19). This text will guide our discussion about the theological depth of our songs. Whether Paul is declaring that we should sing three different categories of songs or is listing synonyms for the same type of songs isn't easy to discern. I am taking the approach that he is declaring three distinct categories. Although I can't prove that, I think the three categories are worthy of discussion. Each category is broader in content than the previous one: Psalms comprise the narrowest category. The hymn category is broader than that of the psalms

---

1. I taught this class as my doctoral project.

but narrower than that of spiritual songs. Spiritual songs comprise the broadest category.

Paul also clarifies that we should "let the word of Christ dwell in us" and that we should be "teaching and admonishing one another in all wisdom" through the songs we sing (Col 3:16). The singing that we do in the church should be filled with the word of God and it should encourage and teach the congregation. There is no question that our singing should magnify and exalt the Lord, as we read in Psalm 34:3; but we are also called to sing to God and to "one another" as well. In other words, our singing has both vertical aspects and horizontal aspects.

TEACHING AND ADMONISHING

Before we discuss the three categories of songs, we should consider Paul's encouragement to "teach and admonish one another in all wisdom, singing psalms and hymns and spiritual songs" (Col 3:16). Interestingly, the CSB inserts the word *through*. It reads, "teaching and admonishing one another *through* psalms, hymns, and spiritual songs" (emphasis mine). Teaching has the sense of conveying truth, while admonishing carries the idea of strong, practical, and moral encouragement.[2] From this passage, we learn that God wants the church to use her music to convey truth and encourage the members. In other words, we should be discipling the congregation through the psalms, hymns, and spiritual songs that we sing.

This is fundamental to the premise of *The Worship Target*. This book challenges church worship ministries to target a growing affection for Christ in worship. We should be helping our congregations grow in their love for Christ through the singing of deep, theological songs. We should be teaching and admonishing them. If that is true, we must find songs that teach and admonish deep theological truth. Let's consider those songs. Let's dive into the psalms.

---

2. Melick states, "Teaching is the orderly arrangement of truth and effective communication of it . . . Admonishing has the element of strong encouragement. It is generally practical and moral, rather than abstract or theological." Melick, *Philippians, Colossians, Philemon*, 304.

PSALMS

I have always loved the psalms; but in 2018, the Lord heightened my interest while I was attending the Getty Sing! Conference, which focused on the psalms. The following year, our worship ministry presented "An Evening with the Psalms," a night of worship that used the psalms for nearly 100 percent of the content. We sang, prayed, and read the psalms. This night was transformative for me and our church. Not only was it a great night, but the addition of the arrangements of the psalms increased the repertoire of songs we could use regularly in Sunday morning worship.

Singing the psalms is clearly instructed in the previously noted Colossians and Ephesians passages. But what exactly was Paul referring to when he taught the Colossian church to sing the psalms? Joseph S. Exell claims, "The psalms, then, which the apostle would have the faithful to sing to one another are those of David, Asaph, and the other sweet singers of Israel."[3] Paul refers to the "inspired Psalms of the Hebrew canon."[4] This is the narrowest category of songs referenced in that passage. When the church sings the psalms, they sing from the songbook of Israel. They sing one of 150 songs inspired by God and placed in the Old Testament. They sing the same songs that Jesus sang.

Little doubt exists that Jesus sang the psalms. D. A. Carson argues that Jesus led the disciples in singing a psalm to conclude the Last Supper in Matthew 26:30.[5] Spurgeon believes Jesus uttered Psalm 22 in its entirety while on the cross: "It may have been actually repeated word by word by our Lord when hanging on the tree; it would be too bold to say that it was so, but even a casual reader may see that it might have been."[6] If Spurgeon is correct, Jesus quoted the entire Psalm 22 on the cross. Moreover, if Jesus were in the habit of singing psalms, he would likely have sung Psalm 22

---

3. Exell, *Philippians–Colossians*, 242.

4. Exell, *Philippians–Colossians*, 242.

5. According to Carson, "The 'hymn' normally sung was the last part of the Hallel (Pss 114–18 or 115–18). It was sung antiphonally. Jesus as the leader would sing the lines, and his followers would respond with 'Hallelujah!' Parts of it must have been deeply moving to the disciples when after the resurrection they remembered that Jesus sang words pledging that he would keep his vows (Ps 116:12–13), and call all nations to praise Yahweh and his covenant love (Ps 117). It may be that Jewish exegesis had already interpreted Psalm 118:25–26 as a reference to Messiah's parousia (Jeremias, *Eucharistic Words*, 255–62)." Carson, *Matthew*, 604.

6. Spurgeon, *The Treasury of David*, 324.

on the cross. Once I know a text as a song, I always sing that text; so, I'm convinced that Jesus sang this psalm on the cross.

Singing the psalms is a rewarding reality for a Christian congregation. After our evening with the psalms, one of our singers came to me and said, "I have always heard that we should sing the psalms, but this is the first time I know what that means." Singing the psalms has not been the tradition in the Southern Baptist churches I have served. I'm trying to change that in my church and have found that these songs have been wholeheartedly received.

Aiding in the acceptance of this change has been the popularization of psalm singing recently by many of the well-known Christian music groups. Shane and Shane have recorded several psalms, and The Brooklyn Tabernacle Choir has arranged and recorded some of the Shane and Shane tunes. G3 Ministries recently published *Psalms and Hymns to the Living God*, which contains a musical setting for each of the 150 psalms. These arrangements are very hymnlike in quality. We also have a host of traditional hymns and contemporary songs based on the psalms. A simple word search for psalms on hymnary.org reveals 24,940 hymn listings that contain references to psalms in their lyrics.[7]

HYMNS

As defined by Merriam-Webster, a hymn is "a song of praise to God, a metrical composition adapted for singing in a religious service, or a song of praise or joy"[8] Hymns are typically biblically inspired. In the New Testament, they were generally, although not always, Hebrew poetic texts such as the psalms. According to Elwell and Beitzel, "logically, most of the hymns found in the NT are based on Hebrew poetic psalm forms, but there is Greek and Latin influence also."[9] In more places than one, Augustine states the essentials of a hymn:[10]

---

7. Zeteo.org and https://contemporarypsalms.blogspot.com/ are good sites for searching for ways to use psalms in worship services.

8. Merriam-Webster.com Dictionary, "hymn."

9. Elwell and Beitzel, "Music and Musical Instruments," 1509.

10. Carter states, "Augustine said: 'Know you what a hymn is? It is a song with praise of God. If you praise God and do not sing, you do not utter a hymn: if you sing and do not praise God, you do not utter a hymn: if you praise anything else, which pertains not to the praise of God, although you sing and praise, you utter no hymn. A hymn then contains these three things, song, and praise, and that of God. Praise then of God in song

1. It must be sung.
2. It must be praise,
3. It must be to God.

These are simple criteria to follow.

In the churches I have served in the past, the title *hymn* was reserved for songs that had stood the test of time and were generally published in the denominational hymnal. These songs could be Reformation hymnody, gospel songs, or psalms, although the church didn't always know they were singing psalms. One of my professors said that a hymn is a song the church sings. I'm uncomfortable with that simple definition because the church may sing songs from time to time that are far from being hymns. If the church sings "Happy Birthday," does that make it a hymn? I hold to Augustine's criteria and define a hymn as a song the church sings that directs praises to God!

The hymns we sing in our churches today come from various sources. I have personally led hymns whose texts were thousands of years old and hymns whose texts were written in the last year. In my church, we don't consider the age of the hymn to determine its fitness for our services. We plan our worship based on the leadership of the Holy Spirit; the sermon being preached that day; and any particular emphasis, such as the Lord's Supper or baptism, that may be a part of the service for the day.

Planning worship without the constraints of whether songs are contemporary or traditional, modern or ancient, is a joyful experience! We choose songs that focus on Christ and help to build gracious and holy affections in the lives of our people. Age and style are of little consideration when determining whether we sing a hymn. Instead, logically and wisely, we base our hymns on biblical texts so that we are careful to stay closely connected to scripture in what we sing.[11]

---

is called a hymn.'" Carter, "9 Things You Should Know," item 9.

11. Some excellent modern sources for hymns are Getty Music and Sovereign Grace Music. These publishers provide deeply theological hymns that are joyful and singable by the congregation. Other companies have picked up on some of these songs and arranged them in ways that make them enjoyable for churches to use. These publishers also produce products for children and home worship.

SPIRITUAL SONGS

Every psalm is both a hymn and a spiritual song. Every hymn is a spiritual song but not necessarily a psalm. A spiritual song, however, is not necessarily a psalm or a hymn. A spiritual song is any song that declares the truth of God's word, communicates the work of God in our lives, and celebrates his power and majesty in our world. I believe that Paul, under the inspiration of the Holy Spirit, was granting some freedom to the church in this category. The Greek word translated "song" is the word *ode*. These songs could be played on an instrument or sung. The fact that Paul placed *pneumatikos* ("spiritual") in front of *ode* is, however, significant. God does not want us to simply sing songs; he wants us to sing spiritual songs. He has, however, given us freedom beyond just singing psalms and hymns. He could have limited our singing to those categories, but he did not. Therefore, we have the freedom from God to sing songs that are spiritual that are not directly from a biblical text, that are not to God but about God and what he's done in our lives. And so, these songs will often be as much about us as they are about God.

Should we vet these songs with scripture? Should they be consistent with scripture? Should they contain a biblical message? Should they be theologically deep? Of course, they should! Interestingly, according to Exell, the word for spiritual songs is the only word of the three (*psalms*, *hymns*, and *spiritual songs*) that makes it into the book of Revelation.[12] Does that mean that we won't sing scripture in heaven? Of course not. In fact, Revelation 15:3 states, "And they sing the song of Moses, the servant of God, and the song of the Lamb, saying, 'Great and amazing are your deeds, O Lord God the Almighty! Just and true are your ways.'"[13] What it does mean is that singing is very important to God, and he is blessed when we do it right. Revelation 14:3 states, "And they were singing a new song before the throne and before the four living creatures and before the elders." What a joy it is for the believer to have a new song in his heart that he can use to exalt Almighty God and his son, Jesus Christ, all in the power of the Holy Spirit!

Spiritual songs is an outstanding category for telling the story of saints who have experienced God's grace in their lives. Ministry songs give a voice to those who have had struggles in their lives and have found the grace of

---

12. According to Exell, "Ὀδή is the only word of this group which the Apocalypse knows (5:9; 14:3; 15:3)." Exell, *Philippians-Colossians*, 243.

13. Exell states, "*Who Were They That Sang?* It is a question of moment for men still." Exell, *Revelation*, 504.

Jesus. Through the songs in this category, we can testify to what the Lord has done in our lives, the church, and our families' lives. However, even though this category offers the most freedom, worship leaders still must be cautious. Because this category isn't directly tied to scripture, we can be tempted to move our focus away from God and toward us. That makes this category dangerous as well as freeing.

One of the roles I provide to my church as worship pastor is vetting our youth's songs. One of the songs that they requested to sing had the words "I," "my," and "me" in it twenty-one times. If the song references me twenty-one times, then who is the song about? That's where the spiritual songs category gets challenging as the temptation exists to sing songs focusing on us rather than focusing on God. Does this category allow us to do so? Yes, it does! That is the beauty of this category. However, what we sing in congregational worship should be primarily about God, and significantly to God. We should balance these realities in our gatherings. If we sing a song focused on God's work in our lives, we should also sing about God's majesty, Christ's atoning act, and the power of the Holy Spirit.

In vetting the songs that fit in this category, we need to consider two things. First, the songs need to be consistent with scripture. We should keep our focus on singing the truth. Often songs will have only one errant phrase, but it is errant nevertheless. Some worship leaders may choose to change that one phrase, but I won't do so.[14] I'd rather not sing the song than shift the writer's original intent. Second, the song needs to be Christ-centered. As an evangelical church, we are focused on the ministry that Christ has in our lives. Therefore, we want to sing songs that declare the beautiful gospel of Jesus Christ.[15] Gospel-rich songs are some of my personal favorites. I can never get enough of singing songs that declare the beauty of Christ's life, death, and resurrection. It's an added bonus if the song also declares Jesus's joyful ascension and the future hope of his return. Every evangelical church should be singing songs that declare the wonderful and beautiful gospel of Jesus Christ!

---

14. US Copyright Office, "Subject Matter and Scope of Copyright," section 102. It is questionable under US Copyright laws to change the lyrics of a song protected under the law.

15. There are many sources for spiritual songs. The Gaithers have been providing songs in this category for six decades. Recently, Charity Gayle gained much popularity in this category. There are many recording artists and publishers that offer music in this category.

THE RIGHT MIX

When we plan worship and select songs in our respective churches, we are all probably starting from different places in our goal of targeting gracious and holy affections for Christ in our worship services. Growing in this process begins by understanding why we are targeting gracious and holy affections in our services rather than passion, sentimentalism, or style. Colossians 3:12–13 reminds us to "put on then, as God's chosen ones, holy and beloved, compassionate [affectionate] hearts, kindness, humility, meekness, and patience, bearing with one another and, if one has a complaint against another, forgiving each other; as the Lord has forgiven you, so you also must forgive." In other words, we are to focus on the holy and gracious affections.

From that foundation, we can begin to understand how to establish the criteria we've discussed in this chapter and the previous one about song selection in our churches. Songs that meet these three criteria (musically beautiful, congregationally singable, and theologically deep) in my church may look different from those in another church. Each worship leader must decide for his church precisely what each of these criteria means. For example, what will it mean to be musically beautiful? What is the congregation capable of singing? What is the faith tradition in the church? This may affect the church's meaning of theologically deep songs.

Regardless of the differences, if we are to grow from being focused on passion and sentimentalism to being genuinely focused on deeply theological songs that lead our congregations to grow in their gracious and holy affections, we must be intentional in our selection process. Currently, we may rely on habits that we have developed over time. Those habits could be singing the same songs we have sung for years, only singing the songs from CCLI's top one hundred, or singing songs from the latest album that dropped on Spotify. We can too easily fall into a pattern, almost as if we have a formula for choosing the songs we sing. The same can be true if we focus on singing psalms, hymns, and spiritual songs. How many psalms, hymns, and spiritual songs belong in each service or for rotating through a month of services? That is a balance that each church will have to determine.

Because my church follows the regulative principle in determining what we include in our worship services, some people reading this may say that we should only sing psalms; but I don't see that principle in scripture.[16]

---

16. See Poythress, "Ezra 3, Union with Christ, and Exclusive Psalmody," 74–94.

Calvin clearly held to the principle of psalm only singing, basing this on 1 Corinthians 14:15: "What am I to do? I will pray with my spirit, but I will pray with my mind also; I will sing praise with my spirit, but I will sing with my mind also." The word used for praise in this text is a version of *psalmos*. Of course, the translation could also read, "I will sing psalms with my spirit." He stated in the preface to the *Genevan Psalter*,

> But what St. Augustine says is true, that none can sing things worthy of God but he who has received power from himself. Wherefore when we have sought all round, searching here and there, we shall find no songs better and more suitable for this end than the Psalms of David which the Holy Spirit dictated and gave to him. And therefore when we sing them, we are as certain that God has put words into our mouths as if he himself sang within us to exalt his glory.[17]

However, the Apostle Paul, also inspired by the Holy Spirit, wrote Colossians and Ephesians; and I hold fast to Colossians 3:16 and live in the freedom that scripture provides.

Even so, I also believe that this text is prescriptive. We are not given the freedom to ignore any of these three categories, as some of our churches are in the habit of doing. Therefore, I suggest that churches sing songs from all three categories regularly, restoring psalm singing to our churches. We will always succeed when singing scripture.

There is no perfect church. Therefore, every church is ripe with growth opportunities. And God has been so kind to us by providing the scripture resources we need to *select theologically rich hymnody* for *church revitalization*. Each change we make in our churches is part of the revitalizing process. Each new direction we take in worship, each new song we sing, and each time we add or remove some element of our worship services is part of the revitalizing process. I encourage you to seek scripture as you discern the Holy Spirit's guidance for the songs you should sing.

---

17. "Men of God," par. 7.

11

Read, Pray, Worship

The LORD your God is with you, he is mighty to save. He will take great delight in you, He will quiet you with his love, He will rejoice over you with singing.
ZEPH. 3:17 (NIV)

IN 2018, I WENT on a mission trip to Ukraine with some good friends who were worship leaders in their churches. We went to teach worship and lead worship at a conference in Kiev for worship leaders and pastors. One of my assignments was teaching a class on leadership. I introduced myself as Brad Newbold, the worship pastor at Concord Baptist Church. That introduction generated the first question of the session: "Worship pastor? What's a worship pastor?" They had never heard the term. Thirty minutes later, we finally got into my material on leadership.

We talked about what a worship pastor is earlier in the book, but let's go a bit deeper. A worship pastor is the person who leads the music in our congregational worship services. He also works with staff to plan and implement various church ministries, including music. Worship leaders go by various titles and may or may not be pastors. That's okay. I'm not in any way attempting to say that everyone who leads the music in our churches must be a pastor. However, I do say that leading worship *is* a pastoral activity. The term *pastor*, as a verb, initially meant "to feed."[1] The verb form is an activity that any Christian can participate in. Anyone can "pastor" or feed people. So, while not everyone who leads the musical worship in our churches is a pastor, each does "pastor" the people as they lead them in

---

1. Merriam-Webster.com Dictionary, "pastor."

congregational worship. I said earlier in chapter 3 that Jesus is our worship leader, and I believe that to be true. But under his leadership, we can pastor the people through music. That said, how do we do that? More specifically, how can we lead to engender gracious and holy affections toward Christ both in ourselves and in our congregations?

PROVIDING SPIRITUAL LEADERSHIP

To provide spiritual leadership, we must first develop and deepen our own spiritual lives. Sometimes as worship leaders, we may believe that our work is spiritual enough; and we fail to work on our own spirituality. But trying to feed others without feeding ourselves leads to burn out. And, yes, finding the time is often difficult. In regular seasons, the pastor should spend time on spiritual growth daily. In those difficult seasons, the pastor's work may overwhelm the opportunity to spend significant time studying the word for personal edification. God grants grace at times like these.

As I write this book, I'm in one of those seasons. I'm spending two hours or more each morning writing before I go to my office at church. Before diving into this intensive writing time, I had spent each morning in the word and prayer. During this time of writing, I have done the same but with a different focus. I have focused my morning prayer and scripture reading on preparation for this book.

In Joshua 7, Joshua had a significant issue to deal with, and God tells Joshua to "get up! Why have you fallen on your face?" (v. 10). God was instructing him to act. Sometimes, we must do the same. So, let's consider some basic guidelines to help us as pastors and worship leaders to remain faithful in our personal spiritual development.

God's Word

First and foremost, we should continue to spend time in God's word. The Bible is an incredible treasure God gave us as a revelation of who he is. Jesus said in John 4:24, "God is spirit, and his worshipers must worship in the Spirit and in truth" (NIV). How can we worship in the Truth if we don't spend time in the word?

My deep appreciation of the Bible has grown significantly in recent years. I love reading the word to my congregation in worship, and I find I have something to share with them if I spend personal time in the Bible.

I love reading the entire Bible each year. There are Bible apps that give us everything we need to accomplish this fantastic feat. My favorite approach is reading the Bible chronologically. Doing so provides a new dimension to the events of the Bible, especially the Old Testament. Continue to set aside time each morning to read the word. I'm sure your life is busy like mine, but if I don't read the Bible in the morning, I rarely find the time later in the day. My wife has been faithful in her morning quiet time for years, but hers is different from mine, as I described earlier in the book. She generally reads the Bible completely through each year, but she is always reading a devotional book as well. She also listens to a sermon from a profoundly theological pastor each morning while she gets ready. This daily discipline prepares her for the challenges that we face in ministry, and I'm convinced this is the reason she is the mature believer that she is.

Not only do we need to set aside time for Bible reading, but we also need to set aside a place. I have a chair in a room in the front of our house where I have my quiet time. It is secluded and peaceful. That's generally my place. When the weather is nice, I move outside to the back deck. Also, a quiet, secluded space. It helps me to have a place that I consistently use each day.

Prayer

Secondly, we must continue to pray. Praying revolutionizes our worship. If we have yet to pray in our private worship, do we have the right to pray in our public worship settings?

I have known several prayer warriors in my lifetime. I wish I were one! I'm not but that doesn't mean I don't love praying. I am continually amazed that the God who created and sustains the universe is willing to hear my prayers. I love praying the prayers of the Bible. One of my favorites is the prayer of Jehoshaphat. He finishes his prayer with these words: "We do not know what to do, but our eyes are on you" (2 Chron 20:12b). I have prayed those words many times.

Many of us follow one of several models of praying. The one that I have found helpful is the acrostic ACTS. This model is an outline to follow during our daily prayer time, guiding us to pray in four categories: adoration, confession, thanksgiving, and supplication.[2]

2. I have known this model for years; but in preparation for this book, I accessed a helpful article at Crosswalk.com. See McMenamin, "What Is the ACTS Prayer Method."

Adoration. Adoration is declaring God's worth as he is. This is our time of prayer where we worship God purely, when we praise him according to his excellent attributes. Our prayers should echo Psalm 103:1: "Bless the LORD, O my soul, and all that is within me, bless his holy name!" When we focus on God's many attributes—holiness, mercy, graciousness, steadfast love, righteousness, and so on—we acknowledge that we worship him for him, not just for what he has done for us. The suggestion here is to follow Jesus's teaching in the The Lord's Prayer. That prayer begins with these words: "Our Father in heaven, hallowed be your name" (Matt 6:9). Jesus suggests that we start by declaring God's holiness. We can then more easily continue by stating more of God's attributes.

Confession. Confessing my sins has never been something I enjoy, but I must do it to be in the right standing with God. First John 1:8–10 makes this clear:

> If we say we have no sin, we deceive ourselves, and the truth is not in us. If we confess our sins, he is faithful and just to forgive us our sins and to cleanse us from all unrighteousness. If we say we have not sinned, we make him a liar, and his word is not in us.

Confessing our sins to God literally provides forgiveness. This prayer is foundational to a holistic Christian life. David expressed this reality in Psalm 32:3–5:

> For when I kept silent, my bones wasted away
>   through my groaning all day long.
> For day and night your hand was heavy upon me;
>   my strength was dried up as by the heat of summer. *Selah*
>
> I acknowledged my sin to you,
>   and I did not cover my iniquity;
> I said, "I will confess my transgressions to the LORD,"
>   and you forgave the iniquity of my sin. *Selah*

As spiritual leaders, we must continue to keep Christ's work in our lives fresh and current. Confessing our sins daily should be part of the discipline that will enable us to lead with spiritual integrity.

Thanksgiving. Thanksgiving is my favorite kind of prayer. I enjoy thanking God for all he has done for me and for blessing me and my family. I also learned very early in my ministry to thank him for the challenging times as well. First Thessalonians 5:18 tells us to "give thanks in all circumstances; for this is the will of God in Christ Jesus for you." There is no better way to cut through the crud in life than by praising God for it. The moment we declare our thanks both *in* the challenge and *for* the challenge, we find God shining through the difficulty. Yes, thanking God in the challenge is easier than thanking him for the challenge; and so, in these times, we need to remember Romans 8:28: "And we know that for those who love God all things work together for good, for those who are called according to his purpose." David also reminds us that the Lord will not forget us in difficult times in Psalm 121:1–4:

> I lift up my eyes to the hills.
>   From where does my help come?
> My help comes from the LORD,
>   who made heaven and earth.
>
> He will not let your foot be moved;
>   he who keeps you will not slumber.
> Behold, he who keeps Israel
>   will neither slumber nor sleep.

God is not sleeping on the job, so we should continue to thank him for all he is doing.

Supplication. Supplication is that part of our prayers where we make requests. Psalm 5:3 encourages us in this: "Morning by morning, O LORD, you hear my voice; morning by morning, I lay my requests before you and wait in expectation" (NIV 1978). Unless you have an NIV Bible that is the 1978 translation, you won't find the rendering "wait in expectation." However, this is how I memorized the verse, and I love the sense that it gives. The modern NIV says, "Wait expectantly," and the ESV renders it, "In the morning, I prepare a sacrifice for you and watch." All of them give the idea of expectation. The beautiful thing about the ACTS approach to prayer is that our requests follow our adoration, confession, and thanksgiving. By the time we get to our requests, God has aligned our hearts with his properly: "Delight yourself in the LORD, and he will give you the desires of your heart" (Ps 37:4). As we delight ourselves in the Lord (by praying in the ACTS model), we also align ourselves with the Lord, allowing God to implant in our hearts the desires that he wishes to fulfill. If God creates the desires in our hearts, then he will grant them.

Worship

Third, we must continue to be worshippers! At CBC, we use an app to organize our worship ministry. One of the cool benefits of that app is we can listen to the songs for the upcoming services. On Sunday mornings, before I go to church, I worship with the songs we will sing that day. Not only am I reminded of the arrangements and the progression of the service, but I focus my heart's affection on Christ in the context of what the church is about to sing. Let's be honest: focusing entirely on God during the congregational worship service is challenging for worship leaders. Having a time of private worship before standing in front of the church is vital to my spiritual life and leadership.

We also need to find times and places to worship God when we are not leading. I remember once we had guest worship leaders for the day at our church, so I was standing with my family singing. My three-year-old daughter looked up at me and said, "Daddy, why are you holding your hands up, and why are your eyes closed?" This moment was excellent for several reasons. First, I could worship freely without any concerns about leading the music. Second, I was able to model singing and worshipping to my young daughter. And third, my church could see me as a worshipper without having to be up front. I encourage every worship leader to find places and times when they are not leaders in the worship context. For example, my wife and I like to join student or college gatherings for worship and enjoy the looks we get when we walk into those settings. Or consider attending another church that has a worship service at a different time from your church. The bottom line is that we need to be worshippers without always having to lead.

Guard Your Heart

Finally, we must continue to guard our hearts. I have known far too many pastors who have failed morally and ended up out of the ministry because they allowed sin to derail their lives. I've seen ministers fail that I considered much more spiritually gifted than I am. None of us are immune to failure! Therefore, we must find someone who will hold us accountable for our actions. We should each have someone in our lives that is always aware of where we are and what we are doing. For those of us who are married, that person can be our spouse. If unmarried, we need to find someone who we are always in touch with and who knows how we spend our time.

When I first surrendered my life to ministry, my pastor told me there were three ministry rules:

1. Never be alone in a room with a woman.
2. Never be alone in a room with a woman.
3. Never be alone in a room with a woman.

I will never ride in a vehicle alone with any woman except my wife. That has created some awkward moments but following that rule has been worth it. I also never keep secrets from my wife. If someone comes to me with something they want to share with me in confidence, I always tell them that whatever they share with me will be shared with my wife. They can then decide if they want to proceed.

Everything I have, I have received from the Lord. The gifts that I use each week to lead our worship team and church are from him. When church musicians begin to believe that we are a "gift to God" as we lead the church in worship, we have forgotten where our abilities get their source. This model of providing spiritual leadership by studying God's word, praying, worshipping, and guarding our hearts will be evident to our churches as we lead them humbly to the throne of God in worship.

RECRUITING A WORSHIP LEADERSHIP TEAM

We must continually recruit teams as leaders of our churches' worship ministries and encourage our teams to help us recruit. I have always encouraged my team members to recruit, and they do, often doing a better job than I do because they usually know more people outside of the church than I do. If you are a team member (praise team singer, instrumentalist in the band or orchestra, or choir member) or leader reading this book, your help in recruiting is essential. Here are a few basic disciplines that will help in recruiting.

Lead the Music Well

Good musicians want to join a well-led group. They hope to participate in a group that looks good, sounds good, and is well-organized. These characteristics become obvious when you hear a group lead and play music. I hired an associate worship pastor based on seeing a video of the church where he was leading. After listening to just one half of the song he led, I was convinced he was the right person for the position. His group looked sharp on stage, they were well organized, and they sounded good.

Leading music well is our number one recruiting tool. Doing so requires making beautiful music that engages the congregation, as discussed in chapter 9. Even if resources are small, we must do our best with what we have. We must be prepared for Sundays if we want others to want to join us.

Recruit, Recruit, Recruit

We must constantly recruit. Every new person we meet should be a recruiting conversation. For me, these conversations occur both in and outside the church. Our worship ministry has many spots that individuals not our church members may fill. Primarily, these are in the choir and orchestra. Individuals in these positions will only sing and play the music the leadership chooses. For other spots, like worship team vocalists, I care deeply that they are church members and have a growing relationship with Christ. My church leadership agrees with my position on recruiting and utilizing non-members, but each church is different. Worship leaders will have to determine that for their settings and ensure the agreement of their church leadership. The point, however, is that worship leaders always need to be recruiting.

Provide What They Need

Musicians need stuff. If they are going to play in the band, they need chord charts or sheet music. They probably need music or iPad stands. If they are singers, they need music and microphones. If they play in the orchestra, they need the right parts in the right keys. They all need to know when rehearsals are. They need to know when the worship services start and when they need to arrive before the service begins. They need a schedule for their participation, if they do not play or sing each week. In many churches, they need words on the wall because they aren't allowed to hold music except in rehearsals. At CBC, they are expected to learn the song but not to memorize the words. And so, the screen on the back wall that they view needs to be the same size as the screen(s) on the front walls that the congregation view.

Let's be honest: musicians are needy people. But some of their needs are legitimate, and as their leaders, we need to provide the things they rightfully need. I have heard it said that an orchestra is like an elephant. We have to provide it space, feed it, and, at the end of the day, clean up the mess! That is true for all musicians. And so, provide what your musicians need or they may be unwilling to remain.

Show Them We Care

My week's most important two hours are Wednesday evenings from 6:00 pm to 8:00 pm when we rehearse. I can't overemphasize the need to bless your musicians during rehearsal. To let you all into my life a bit, I go home early on Wednesday afternoons and rest. I usually take a nap. I've found that I am much more demanding if I'm tired at rehearsal. If I am rested, I am much more patient and understanding. That rest time is far more important than anything I might do in the office on Wednesday afternoons. I know that not all of us have that luxury, but the point is that we need to be kind to our musicians during rehearsal. We need to show them that we care about them. I also try to provide more than music for those at rehearsal. I'm notorious for my bad dad jokes in rehearsal and try to offer a word of spiritual encouragement out of my week.

Also, show that you care away from the church. Find ways to connect when people are sick or have had a family loss. Being there for a family in difficult times will significantly grow our relationships. Show love and encouragement in times of celebration as well. There's nothing better than celebrating significant life events with the members of our teams.

SETTING OUR GOALS FOR WORSHIP RENEWAL

For a conference session I taught recently, I developed this purpose statement:

> The purpose of this seminar is to help congregations and leaders identify and distinguish between worship that stirs their emotive passions or sentimental idealism versus worship that stirs gracious and holy affections. This will help believers understand that one goal (perhaps the primary goal) of biblical worship is to stir the worshipper's true affection for Christ.[3]

3. Newbold, "Worship Strategy for Renewal."

We have previously identified that the target of our worship should be gracious and holy affections for Christ. But what does that entail? How do we get from where we are in worship to where we want to be? How do we revitalize our worship services to engender gracious and holy affections for Christ in our congregations?

Any time we plan a transformation in our worship services, we must first set a goal. Where are we headed? Once chosen, every decision needs to focus on that goal. Suppose we are to grow our congregations in worshipping with gracious and holy affections. In that case, we must be intentional about doing so: intentional in how we order our worship services, in the songs we play and sing, in the scriptures we read, in the prayers we offer, and even in the way we use the technology we have. Everything that we do from the platform disciples the people that we lead. When we disciple them well, we will produce disciples who desire to worship Christ in Spirit and Truth with their heart's affections set on him. When we disciple them poorly, we will make disciples who believe that worship should be targeted toward their preferences.

For some of us, the changes we need to make to target gracious and holy affections may be few, fine-tuning what we already do in our services. Others may need to make significant changes in how they have traditionally conducted worship. When that is the case, I strongly recommend doing so incrementally, using a pastoral approach. Whatever the process or the speed of these changes in our worship services, we should continually look to the scriptures for answers. We should worship God in Spirit and Truth, and that truth should come from the word of God.

Shepherding and pastoring our people are as essential as the result. The journey often provides growth. We may never get the desired results if done too quickly or harshly. Seven years ago, when I first came to CBC, I realized that although powerful and beautiful, many of the services had as their target the stirring of the congregation's passions. Members were encouraged to respond physically to the music, clapping, applauding, and giving standing ovations after choir and orchestra numbers. Getting such responses had become the driving force behind the music ministry to the point that the music in any given service often overwhelmed the church's affection for Christ. Slowly, over the course of these past seven years, we have transformed our worship services into ones that are more discipleship-based services that target gracious and holy affections. (By the way, we still have work to do!)

The effect of doing so slowly rather than radically changing the church's expectations overnight hit me after a recent Sunday morning service. I realized that the songs we had sung that day were all songs or arrangements that the church did not know seven years ago, yet no one complained regarding the musical choices. The church had been discipled and learned these songs over time. We must love our people enough to make essential changes over time, allowing our congregations to understand the scriptural foundation for the changes and become accustomed to the new without degrading or criticizing the old.

ACCEPTING THE CHALLENGE

When worship leaders commit to this process, they will face challenges. Every church has a set of beliefs about worship. Some believe that we need to sing the songs of our grandparents' generation because they evoke such warm, sentimental feelings. Others think we need to pump up the jam so that the whole congregation will get engaged in physical expression in worship and express our passions. Some want to cherry-pick songs from Christian radio to plan worship services. When we refocus our worship services and realign ourselves with scripture, attempting to grow gracious and holy affections for Christ through worship, our congregations will miss what they have been used to. Over time, their expectations will change and the difference will be noted. I've had new attendees at our church tell me that there is something distinctive about our worship even though they can't precisely identify that difference. As the ones designing the worship experiences for our churches, what greater calling could we have than to help our churches focus on growing affection for Christ?

12

For The Small Church

His master said to him, "Well done, good and faithful servant. You have been faithful over a little; I will set you over much. Enter into the joy of your master."
MATTHEW 25:21

MOST PEOPLE BELIEVE CHURCH size is a big deal or a small deal, depending on your perspective. And most believe it is a massive deal as it relates to worship. People may think that leading a congregation of hundreds or thousands significantly differs from leading a church of seventy-five or fewer. They may also believe that leading the worship team (or leading alone with no team) will radically differ in a large or small church. But the reality is that leading worship is leading worship.

I have led worship in all sorts of situations. I have led services with as few as fifteen and with as many as fifteen hundred. Quite honestly, I don't remember it being that much different. Maybe a little harder on the nerves on one end and a little harder to staff on the other; but honestly, standing up in front of a group of people singing praise to God and asking them to join you is similar, regardless of the group size. If you can lead the small group, I am confident you can lead the large group.

My first church was in a rural community of dairy farmers. It was a good church with good people. Janis and I often went to our car after church to find two bags of groceries in the back seat. It was common for us to eat Sunday lunch with one of those families each week, and those families knew how to cook! We averaged about one hundred in worship; and on a really good day, we would have a choir of about twenty singers.

The Worship Target

We had an organ and a piano, but we were still waiting for someone to play the organ. The pianist was good, but she could only play in a few keys. If my memory serves me right, she could play in one or two sharps and one, two, or three flats. So, we only sang hymns that were in those keys. She was the regular pianist. We would sing three hymns, a choir special, and an invitation hymn each Sunday. Eventually, we started adding scripture songs. We would present two cantatas[1] a year and used accompaniment tracks for those. That's my small church experience. I'm not in any way attempting to say that I know your situation, but I have had the privilege of serving in multiple sizes of churches. Each one had its own set of unique challenges.

This book is for every church. My most recent experiences are from larger churches, so my examples throughout the book relate to those situations. However, the principles I relay in this book are not limited to a large church. They aren't restricted to contemporary, traditional, or modern. They are appropriate to any church that desires to help its people grow in gracious and holy affections for Christ. Any church can apply these principles to her situation. The question for this chapter is, how do you do that in a small(er) church?

First, let's look at simple descriptions of churches of different sizes. These aren't from my research, but they are helpful:[2]

1. A small church has 0 to 99 attendees; it represents 59 percent of all churches in the USA. There are 177,000 of them and include 9 million worshippers in total. These churches generally have one pastor who is often part-time or bi-vocational, sometimes full-time.

2. Medium small churches have 100 to 499 attendees, representing 35 percent of all churches. There are 105,000 of them and include 25 million worshippers. The staffing varies from one to five pastors, either part-time or full-time.

3. Medium churches have 500 to 999 attendees, representing 4 percent of churches. There are 12,000 medium churches nationwide that include 9 million worshippers. They generally have a large staff who oversee volunteers.

---

1. A collection of songs that are organized according to a theme, usually around Christmas and Easter.
2. Watson, "Worship in the Average Church in America," paras. 1–12.

4. Large churches have 1,000 to 1,999 attendees, representing 2 percent of all churches. There are 6,000 of these churches that include 8 million worshippers. They also have many paid staff.

5. Megachurches have 2,000 to 9,999 attendees, representing 0.5 percent of all churches. There are 1,170 megachurches that include 4 million worshippers. These churches have from twenty to over one hundred full-time paid pastors and multi-million-dollar budgets.

6. Super mega (or giga) churches have over 10,000 attendees; they represent 0.01 percent of all churches. There are 50 giga churches in the US that include 700,000 worshippers.

As Watson notes, "The average church in America is small. They have limited staff and limited resources in both musicians, production, and sound. Despite their limitations, these small and medium-small churches serve far more people than the super-mega churches, mega-churches, and large churches combined."[3] Understanding this is essential. The significance of the small to medium-sized church should not be overlooked. Most evangelicals in the United States attend one of these churches when they gather with other believers. Think of it this way: if you took every super mega church in America, you could fill Arrowhead Stadium in Kansas City ten times. If you took every small and medium-sized church, you could fill Arrowhead Stadium 485 times! It is time for us to recognize the significance of small and medium-sized churches.

If you are reading this, I assume you serve a church that falls into the small to medium categories. This book is for you. Consider our opportunities as worship leaders in small churches to impact the world for Christ. Consider the 43 million believers who attend our churches weekly. We can significantly influence the kingdom as we lead our churches in worship. So, how do we lead small church members to grow in gracious and holy affections for Christ?

I see three key areas where we can implement *The Worship Target* in small to medium-sized churches. First, we must embrace a vision for the worship ministry in our churches. Second, we need to select good songs and plan good services. Third, we must lead them well, designing our services to engage in robust congregational singing.

---

3. Watson, "Worship in the Average Church in America." para. 11.

EMBRACE THE VISION

Solomon wrote in the book of Proverbs, "Where there is no vision, the people perish" (Prov 29:18a KJV). Every area of ministry will benefit from a clearly articulated vision. This is true for preaching, youth, and senior adult ministries, and it is definitely true for worship and music ministries. What is the vision for your worship ministry? If you are scratching your head, I get it. Many of us never stop to think this through. Let's think it through together. Sometime, when no one else is in the church building, walk in and look around. Start in the back of the room where most people sit on Sundays and look at the front of the room where the pulpit, platform, maybe the choir loft, and the microphones reside. Visualize what you would love that space to look like on Sunday mornings (assuming that's when you usually meet). What would you like to see? If it were me, I would visualize musicians filling that platform. Maybe a pianist, a guitarist, someone playing a cajón, djembe, or drum set. I would envision a few singers singing into a microphone; for me, there would be whatever size choir that would fit. Whatever you envision as you stand at the back of the sanctuary, begin praying for it. Begin asking God if he would bless your church with a growing worship ministry. Right now, it may be just you and no other help; but let's pray that God would change that. In fact, I encourage you to ask your church to pray with you. When we pray, we see God work. When we pray and see success, we have another reason to worship God for his kind generosity and blessings.

Now, move to the front of the room. Stand where the worship leader or pastor would generally stand. Look out across the pews or chairs in the room. Picture the dream in your mind. What would you wish for this coming Sunday? If it were me, I would want a congregation full of people worshipping God, centered on Jesus Christ, and empowered by the Holy Spirit. So, let's pray that God would fill this room with people singing the gospel's profound truths each week.

Now, what will we sing? As you walk around the worship center, what do you visualize the church singing? And what do you visualize happening between those songs? Can you think through the content of what you want your church to sing? I suggest that you would like to sing triumphant songs focused on God the Father. Songs that declare God's faithfulness, holiness, power, glory, love, and majesty. I also suggest that you would want to sing songs that tell the gospel story. These songs declare who Jesus Christ is and what amazing things he has done. Then, you may consider singing songs that celebrate the Holy Spirit's work in our lives. Finally, as a church, we may envision singing spiritual songs telling our redemption story. Between those songs, how powerful would it be to include scripture readings and prayers that encourage the church beyond what the songs alone can do?

We can write a vision statement together, if you are tracking with me. Taking in the hopes and dreams of our walk through the sanctuary and our view of what we may sing, read, and pray in our services, our vision statement may be something like this: "The vision of the ABC Church worship ministry is that we grow a music team to lead the congregation to sing songs glorifying God the Father, the Lord Jesus Christ, in the power of the Holy Spirit sharing scripture and prayers supporting those songs." This statement may seem too simple to you, or it may seem too lofty to you; but it can serve as an example of what a vision statement may look like for the worship ministry of your church. You may say, "But wait! I don't have a worship ministry!" I get it. But if you are reading this book, God has given you an assignment. He expects you to act in some way to help grow your church's musical worship, and the best way to start is by casting the vision.

Once God has shown you your vision, you must communicate it. I have been telling my church for years that we sing songs that are (1) musically beautiful, (2) congregationally singable, and (3) theologically deep. I cast that vision to them regularly. As you share your vision, ask the church to pray with you. When God answers their prayers, announce that to them and let the entire church celebrate the wins. One Sunday, I asked the church to pray for a specific need in our worship ministry. By that evening, I had a phone call from someone offering to fill the need. Answers don't usually happen that fast or that easily, but often the church knows someone who may be able to fill the need. Asking them to pray with you gets them on board to see how God may work to answer that request.

FIND GOOD RESOURCES

To select good songs, we must find sources that will meet the theological criteria we establish for our churches and find music that our worship ministries can attain. Where can I find good, theologically profound songs that my church can sing, my pianist or guitarist can play, and I can lead? That is a good question. But you may also be asking, where can I find a pianist or guitarist? Let's start with that one.

Find Musicians

Finding musicians for our churches is challenging. Recently, at a conference I taught, a man asked, "But what do I do if I don't have a pianist?" So, what do you do if you have no instrumental musicians in your church who are willing to play to accompany your church's worship service? First, consider that you didn't get here overnight unless you're a brand-new church with no instrumentalists. Most churches had accompanists of some kind at some point in their history, and those people have left or passed away over time. When churches reach this point, it is generally because they haven't invested in the next generation of musicians or allowed young people to play in church. I get that. It's hard to turn things over to less gifted, younger musicians; but if you don't, you will eventually have no musicians in the church. And then you find yourself in a tough spot.

First, churches must begin investing in the next generation of musicians. Find someone in your community who is giving piano or guitar lessons and ask if their best student could come and play once a month. Go to schools and ask the music teacher who they recommend. Go to all the music concerts in your area, even a county fair where some bands are playing. Ask them if any of the band members are willing to come and play at your church or if they know someone who would. Musicians know musicians. Nearly every community has an informal network of musicians. We regularly find musicians through the network of vocalists and instrumentalists in our town.

Second, if you have no one to accompany your church's singing, you may have to find a way to use a prerecorded accompaniment option. A digital hymnal is one option. This device comes preloaded with hymn accompaniment. You can buy one with the most popular hymnals already installed. If you are in this situation but prefer more modern music, you have several options. Do a quick Google search for "worship backing tracks," and several options appear. Options like *Worship Backing Band* and *MultiTracks* are options. These offer more flexibility as you can turn specific instruments in the band on and off. They are primarily subscription-based and will require a bit more technological knowledge. The good thing about backing tracks is that as you add live instrumentalists, you can still use the tracks and turn off the instruments in the tracks of those musicians who begin coming to help lead worship.

Let me share some thoughts on style as it relates to finding musicians. I have argued in this book that style doesn't really matter. What matters is the heart of the lyrics of the song. We want to sing songs that will lead our congregations to grow in gracious and holy affections for Christ. But what if you have found an accompanist—a guitarist, pianist, or organist—and they are limited in their style? I say go with that style. (For now!) If a pianist or organist can only play hymns traditionally, but they do it well, then sing traditional hymnody. If you find a guitarist who only plays modern or contemporary songs, go with it. My mom was in a church that sang with DVDs. Then they found a young man who could play guitar and sing, but he led more modern music. My mom loved the fact that they had a real, live worship leader! He blessed that church, even though they had to change their singing style. Perhaps those musicians can eventually expand their repertoires.

Find Good Songs

Finding good songs can be as difficult as finding good musicians. To help our churches move forward theologically in congregational worship, we need to sing good songs. To sing good songs, we need to find good songs. Finding good songs means avoiding problematic songs. If we only sing songs that arouse sentimentality or our passions, then we need to find different songs. They don't have to be new in the sense of having been written recently, but they may need to be new to the rotation of songs that your church sings. By the way, many churches sing too many songs, not each Sunday but overall. I have a friend who tries to keep his selection list of active songs for his church down to fifty. I don't keep my list that small, but limiting the number for your church may help improve congregational singing because the people will have a chance to get familiar with what you sing. Here are some sources of songs that may help.

The hymnal. The hymnal is a source of great songs. Keep looking and cling to the ones that effectively meet the criteria of being musically beautiful, congregationally singable, and theologically profound. You may have to limit singing those songs that target passion and sentimentality. Most churches only sing a fraction of the songs in their hymnals. You may have hundreds of songs they have never sung right before you. Dig into the hymnal and find the treasures there. There will be good, biblically supported songs in any hymnal. Particularly, look for hymns that are based on the psalms. Use the resources within the hymnal such as the index, responsive readings, and medley suggestions. Try to find songs that express worship to the triune God. Our worship services should be trinitarian. We should sing to and about God the Father and God the Son and in the power of God the Holy Spirit.

Online resources. When I first began in music ministry, life was simple; at least finding music was. We had the hymnal, which was our only resource for congregational singing. For our choirs, we had collections, individual octavos, and denominationally produced music magazines such as *Glory Songs,* which were great sources of choir music. Today, we have PraiseCharts, Lifeway Worship, SongSelect, Getty Music, Sovereign Grace Music, and several other online publishers for congregational music. We have Prism Music, Brentwood Benson, Word, Semsen Music, CCT Music, and many others for the choir. These publishers produce a wide variety of styles of music suited to various choir sizes. The challenge for each of us is finding the music that works for us and our situations.

I suggest narrowing the search for congregational music to as few sources as possible. If you are part-time or volunteer, I strongly recommend you find a simple approach that will work for you. Utilize three primary sources to find music to target growing gracious and holy affections in your church: a source for traditional hymns, a source for modern hymns, and a source for your choir, if you have one.

Traditional hymns. First, I would find a good online source for traditional hymns. (By the way, many modern hymns are being written, and we will discuss them next.) The instrumentation that you have in your church will somewhat determine the best place to find hymns. If you have a pianist who is your primary instrumentalist and he or she reads music, use the hymnal. Most pianists can read hymns easily, and many are adept at improvising on those hymns. If you lead primarily with guitar or a pianist who only plays by ear or chord charts, I would find another source for your hymns. PraiseCharts or SongSelect from CCLI are excellent options. PraiseCharts is the more flexible option because of the vast number of resources it offers. The good news is that many artists are recording hymn or psalm projects, and PraiseCharts will have all the music you need for those projects. Many of these projects are modern adaptations of traditional hymns; but generally, congregations used to singing traditional hymns can adapt quickly. I wouldn't abandon traditional hymns entirely, but I don't say that because "the old hymns have such good theology," which is what I often hear. Some old hymns have good theology; others have lousy theology. I suggest using traditional hymnody because it connects people to the church's traditions. Many guests to your church will have some familiarity with traditional hymnody. Abandon the old hymns that are theologically weak and sing the strong hymns with conviction.

Modern hymns. The most exciting development in church music has been the modern hymn movement. I remember the first time I led the powerful hymn *Power of the Cross* at the Missouri Baptist Convention annual meeting. When we finished, the president of the convention asked me, "What was that?" When I told him it was a modern hymn, he turned to his music minister and said, "Let's sing that at our church!" Songs like *In Christ Alone, 10,000 Reasons, Amazing Grace (My Chains are Gone), His Mercy Is More, Before the Throne of God Above, Come Behold the Wondrous Mystery,* and others have become staples worldwide. These songs provide a breath of fresh singing to the church with deeply theological lyrics and beautiful and generally attainable music.

Modern hymns are available on several online websites. PraiseCharts, as mentioned previously, and SongSelect are good sources. You can also go directly to Getty Music or Sovereign Grace Music to find music to purchase. Keith Getty announced at the recent Getty Sing! Conference that they will produce a hymnal. This should be an excellent resource for churches of all sizes to sing theologically rich music from a type of product many churches are comfortable using. Getty Music also produces kids' hymns for children's choirs and family worship.

Psalm singing. We discussed psalm singing in chapter ten, so I won't go in-depth except to help with resources for the small church. I believe we should sing the psalms, but how do we do that? The first place to start is in your hymnal. In the back is a scriptural index showing which hymns have a psalm in the text. Another great resource is hymnary.org. You can search for any psalm and discover the hymns based on that psalm. For example, this morning, I searched for Psalm 150. In that search, I found several hymns. So, traditional hymns are one source of psalm singing.

You can also find a wide variety of psalms from new resources. G3 Publishing has recently published *Psalms and Hymns to the Living God.*[4]

---

4. Aniol et al., *Psalms and Hymns for the Living God.*

This psalter hymnal will be playable by pianists who are comfortable playing traditional hymns. On Planning Center, search for psalms and many options will appear. Some are great and others are too challenging for most congregations to sing. However, you can listen to them and get an idea of what will work in your situation.

Plan the Service

Planning the service is as important as the songs you choose to sing. In chapter 8, I listed our regular service order, so I won't repeat that here. Keep these things in mind as you plan:

- Try to isolate worship from other things that have to happen in your entire service. For example, if you must share announcements, keep them either at the very beginning, before the opening prayer or song, or at the very end after the conclusion of the sermon or invitation time. Doing so helps the congregation to keep the worship time pure.

- Make sure that you read scripture in addition to the scripture for the sermon. Plan for scripture readings as worship events just as you would a song. Plan for many opportunities to pray.

- Plan a lot of prayer during worship services. I suggest these three key moments for prayer. First, pray at the beginning of the service. This prayer should focus on asking for God's help to lead us through the service. Pray for the worship team and pastor as they lead us. Traditionally, this is called the prayer of invocation, asking for God's blessing and presence in the service. The second natural time to pray is between the music and the sermon. In our services, I pray that prayer. I intentionally pray a transition from what we have just sung to move into a time of worship focused on the word of God. The third place to pray is at the end of the sermon. Our pastor prays that prayer each week. We also plan other times for prayer in our services as the need arises.

LEAD WELL

Choosing good songs and planning a good service is the start. Following that, you must lead well:

- Lead with confidence. Know the song and sing it with boldness. Congregations want to sing, but they don't want to stand out when they do so. If we lead confidently, they can follow us and not feel self-conscious.
- Don't say unnecessary things. If the text of a song is strong, it will need minimal introduction.
- Be prepared. If you are going to speak between songs say something meaningful and don't make it up on the fly. Also, don't ramble. Say what you're going to say and move on. Think through the service and know what you are going to do. One time, I was in a service where the worship leader started by saying that he was supposed to share the announcements, but he didn't have a bulletin. So, he had to ask someone to give him a bulletin. That was very distracting.
- Be ready and move from one element to the next with as little disruption as possible.
- Be as familiar with your pastor's sermon as possible. I am blessed. My pastor gives me one year's worth of sermon titles and texts ahead of time. That is very helpful when planning. You probably don't get that. But take what you know and apply it to your plan and leadership.
- Rehearse. Rehearsing is essential, and I ensure I am well-rehearsed before Sunday morning. I also go back over the songs in my quiet time early on Sunday morning. I worship before I get to church. This helps align my heart to what I believe God will do that day.

Prepare well and lead well. Then get out of the way and let God work.

RECOMMISSION THE CHOIR

If you have a choir or plan to start one, I recommend using it primarily as a worship-leading choir.[5] I can't fully explain what that means here; but briefly, a worship-leading choir is a choir whose primary purpose is to lead congregational worship. They don't just exist to sing choir features or specials. At rehearsal, they don't just rehearse the special for the coming week; they rehearse everything the church will sing that Sunday. Doing so does two things: it prepares the choir to lead the church, and it turns evening

---

5. Do you have a choir? My father-in-law is in his late 80s and still preaches every Sunday. (He's my hero!) He pastors a small church that averages about fifteen in worship. They have a choir every week! If they can have a choir, so can you!

rehearsals into worship services. Making this change revolutionized our choir ministry and allowed the choir to serve as a training ground for worship team singers.

If you follow this plan, most of the music you teach your choir will be music you will teach your congregation. That means you don't need dedicated choir music. However, I have found if you want to grow a choir, you must challenge them with good choir music as well. Periodically, have them sing some songs that are special to them. You can then use that music for Easter, Christmas, or worship nights. Learning music for special events can also give you great music throughout the year. Sources for the music for those special events come from Prism Music,[6] Brentwood Benson, CCT Music, Word, and others. I always look for theologically robust, challenging, and potentially congregationally singable songs for my choir.

Most of the special music that our choir sings ends up being sung by our congregation. That way, I get a double bang for my dollars spent and rehearsal time. I also use the same sources for the choir as I do for the congregation. You can focus a year of choir specials on songs you want your congregation to learn. Teach them to your choir and praise team (if you have one) first and present them as specials. Then ask your congregation to join you in subsequent weeks. Whenever our choir sings a feature, I tell the congregation they can join. One week, I saw a video on Facebook that a mom took of her ten-year-old son singing loudly and proudly along with the choir special. What an encouragement to know that kind of engagement with the choir!

CONCLUSION

Let me encourage you: what you do is essential! And there is always work to do. Whether we lead congregations of five or five thousand, we must always work to accomplish the work of worship leadership. And there are no small worship services. Maybe the numbers aren't huge; but to God, every worship experience is one more time that a group of individuals gets to know and experience the greatness of God's kindness and mercy. Pursue him with everything you have!

---

6. Prism Music travels the country annually hosting Prism Music Previews that allow you to hear and see their latest choir music. These are fun events and well worth your time.

13

Final Words

I SERVED IN A group composed of worship leaders from various parts of our state called the Regional Worship Consultants. We had already had several meetings when a new guy joined the group. At his first meeting, he sat at a corner of the large rectangular table we were all sitting around. Our meeting began at about nine in the morning. By the time we were about to break for lunch, the new guy still hadn't said a word. He finally spoke up and said that he had thoroughly enjoyed the meeting because he hadn't known there were others who thought like him. He was an effective worship leader in his church, but he felt isolated.

If you are the worship leader in your church, you may feel the same way. No one else in your church or your staff thinks like you do. Probably no one else in your family feels like you do. You desire to lead your church in pure, holy worship, but they don't get it. You are not alone. Others of us feel the same way.

Let me encourage you. First, find a group where you can spend time with others who feel like you do about worship. Attend a conference, a music publisher's reading session, or a denominational convention. Have lunch with another worship leader in your town periodically, even if they come from a different denomination or theological background. Find someone you may call regularly to bounce ideas off of, even if they live across the state or country. In other words, make a friend with someone who thinks like you.

Second, consider taking classes. Participating in a class at the closest seminary or college that offers courses in worship can be life changing. I was on the fence about pursuing my doctorate when a friend told me if you do it, in three years, you'll have it. If you don't, in three years, you won't. It was great advice. Even though it took me more like four years, it was well worth my time. And I made great friends along the way.

Finally, know in your heart that what you are doing is the greatest work in the world. God has created us to worship him and to give him glory. You have the privilege each Sunday to usher your church into God's throne room. There is no more excellent endeavor in life than leading the church in worship. And, although perhaps the most challenging task God will ever assign you, it is the most rewarding. Stay with it and be aware that you will be blessed and that you are a blessing!

What a journey this has been! If you have made it this far, I'm grateful for you. God has truly blessed me through this process. *The Worship Target* is an assignment God gave me in 1989; however, I didn't know it then. Thank you for reading. I hope that God will bless you and your church through these pages. And if you need help, I would love to come alongside you and your church. You can reach me at theworshiptarget@gmail.com

I am grateful that Christ has called me to his side to do the work that is truly his. I am forever grateful that he called me as his under shepherd in the task of calling the church to him through worship for these forty years. I can't wait to see what he has in store next.

> *Now to him who is able to do far more abundantly than all that we ask or think, according to the power at work within us, to him be glory in the church and in Christ Jesus throughout all generations, forever and ever. Amen. (Eph 3:20–21)*

APPENDIX

Resources

Music Publishers

- Lifeway Worship (https://worship.lifeway.com/)

  Lifeway provides an a la carte approach to purchasing music for your praise band, choir, and orchestra. They have current songs and arrangements of hymns that play and sing well.

- Prism Music (https://prismmusic.com/)

  Prism provides powerful arrangements of contemporary worship songs and classic hymns in collections. They have regional reading sessions that you can attend and hear the music demonstrated.

- Brentwood Benson Music (https://brentwoodbenson.com/)

  Brentwood Benson provides a vast array of musical collections and individual titles for all church music ministries.

- Little Big Stuff Music (https://littlebigstuff.com/)

  Little Big Stuff produces children's musicals that are great for your kids' music camp or weekly kids' music program.

- Sovereign Grace Music (https://sovereigngracemusic.com/)

  Sovereign Grace provides fresh, theologically rich music for the church. They also periodically produce children's music products.

- Getty Music (https://www.gettymusic.com/)

  Getty Music provides new, theologically rich hymnody for the church. They produce children's music and albums. They also organize and lead the annual Getty Sing! Conference.

- G3 Ministries (https://g3min.org/library-resources/hymnal/)

  G3 is not a music publisher, but they have produced a hymnal that includes all 150 of the psalms set to music in a hymn-like structure.

- Semsen Music (https://semsenmusic.com/)

  Semsen produces a full line of church music resources.

- CCT Music (https://www.cctmusic.com/)

  CCT provides recording services for your choir and they publish music for the choir and orchestra. They are particularly known for their Christmas collections.

- Praise Charts (https://www.praisecharts.com/)

  Praise Charts provides praise band/team and orchestral arrangements for modern worship music. Most major artists will be found on Praise Charts.

Websites/Technology

- Planning Center (https://home.planningcenteronline.com/)

  Planning Center provides a website and app-based approach to organizing your worship ministry and library. You can plan your worship services and schedule your team through this app.

- ProPresenter (https://renewedvision.com/propresenter)

  ProPresenter is a presentation software to present lyrics and videos to your congregation.

RESOURCES

Technology

- Allen & Heath (https://www.allen-heath.com/)

  A&H provides resources for live sound, installed sound, and music production.

- Shure (https://www.shure.com/en-US)

  Shure provides state of the art microphones and wireless systems for the church.

- Ultimate Ears (https://pro.ultimateears.com/)

  UE provides custom in-ear monitors.

- Paragon 360 (https://paragon360.com/)

  Paragon 360 provides a full range of services for the church, including design and installation for worship centers.

- Yamaha (https://usa.yamaha.com/products/musical_instruments/pianos/grand_pianos/index.html).

  Yamaha provides world class grand pianos and other instruments.

- Nord (https://www.nordkeyboards.com/)

  Nord keyboards provide digital keyboards for the church.

- ETC Lighting (https://www.etcconnect.com/)

  ETC provides lighting resources for the church and theater.

Bibliography

Allen, David L. *Hebrews*. The New American Commentary 35. Nashville: B&H, 2010.
Aniol, Scott. "Biblical Foundations." Lecture presented at Southwestern Baptist Theological Seminary, Fort Worth, TX, January 12, 2016.
———. *Changed from Glory into Glory*. Peterborough, ON: Joshua, 2023.
Aniol, Scott, et al., eds. *Psalms and Hymns for the Living God*. China: G3 Ministries, 2023. https://g3min.org/library-resources/hymnal/.
Aquinas, Thomas. *Summa Theologica*. Pt. 1 Vol. I QQI-XXVI. Translated by the Fathers of the English Dominican Province. London: Burns Oates & Washbourne, n.d. Logos Bible Software.
Augustine, Aurelius. *The City of God* 1. Edited by Marcus Dodd. Edinburgh: T & T Clark, 1871. Project Gutenberg, 2014. https://gutenberg.org/files/45304/45304-h/45304-h.htm/.
Augustine of Hippo. *The Trinity*. Edited by Hermigild Dressler. Translated by Stephen McKenna. The Fathers of the Church 45. Washington, DC: Catholic University of America, 1963. Logos Bible Software.
Bargatze, Nate. "Stand Up Monologue." *Saturday Night Live*. October 28, 2023. http://youtube.com/watch?v=ED5RX-fou34/.
Begg, Alistair. "Pastor, You Are Not the Worship Leader." Sermon delivered at Getty Sing! Conference, Nashville, TN, September 4, 2024.
Bergen, Robert D. *1, 2 Samuel*, The New American Commentary 7. Nashville: Broadman & Holman, 1996.
Bernard of Clairvaux. *On Loving God*. Coppell, TX: Cassia, 2009.
Block, Daniel I. *For the Glory of God: Recovering a Biblical Theology of Worship*. Grand Rapids: Baker Academic, 2014.
Borchert, Gerald L. *John 1–11*. The New American Commentary 25A. Nashville: Broadman & Holman, 1996.
Calvin, John. *Institutes of the Christian Religion* 1. Edited by John T. McNeill. Translated by Ford Lewis Battles. The Library of Christian Classics. Louisville: Westminster John Knox, 1960. Logos Bible Software.
Carson, D. A. *Matthew*. The Expositor's Bible Commentary. Revised Edition. Edited by Tremper Longman III and David E. Garland. Grand Rapids: Zondervan, 2010.
Carter, Joe. "Things You Should Know about Christian Hymns." TGC. September 22, 2018. https://www.thegospelcoaliton.org/article/9-thing-know-christian-hymns/.

Bibliography

Clarke, Samuel. *A Discourse concerning the Unchangeable Obligations of Natural Religion and the Truth and Certainty of the Christian Revelation.* London: James Knapton, 1706.

Clement of Alexandria. *The Stromata, or Miscellanies.* Book II. Edited by Peter Kirby. Earlychristianwritings.com, 2001-2022. http://www.earlychristianwritings.com/text/clement-stromata-book2.html/.

Cross, F. L., and Elizabeth A. Livingstone, eds. *The Oxford Dictionary of the Christian Church.* New York: Oxford University Press, 2005.

Descartes, René. *The Passions of the Soul.* Translated and annotated by Stephen Voss. Indianapolis: Hackett, 1989.

Dixon, Thomas. "'Emotion': The History of a Keyword in Crisis." *Emotion Review* 4 (2012) 338–44.

———. *From Passions to Emotions: The Creation of a Secular Psychological Category.* Cambridge: Cambridge University Press, 2003.

Duignan, Brian. "Enlightenment." *Encyclopedia Britannica.* https://www.britannica.com/event/Enlightenment-European-history/.

Edwards, Jonathan. *Religious Affections.* Lexington, KY: Feather Trail, 2009.

Elwell, Walter A., and Barry J. Beitzel. "David." *Baker Encyclopedia of the Bible* 1. Grand Rapids: Baker, 1988, 581–586.

———. "Music and Musical Instruments." *Baker Encyclopedia of the Bible* 2. Grand Rapids: Baker, 1988, 1508–1512.

Exell, Josheph S. *Philippians–Colossians.* The Biblical Illustrator 2. New York: Fleming H. Revell, n.d.

———. *Revelation.* The Biblical Illustrator 23. London: James Nisbet, n.d.

Forney, Kristine, et al. *The Enjoyment of Music.* 14th ed. New York: W. W. Norton, 2020.

Foster, Richard. "The Four Degrees of Love: Bernard of Clairvaux." *Devotional Classics: Selected Readings for Individuals and Groups.* Edited by Richard J. Foster and James Bryon Smith. New York: Harper Collins, 1993, 40–45.

Grudem, Wayne. *Systematic Theology: An Introduction to Biblical Doctrine.* Grand Rapids: Zondervan, 1994.

Hall, Travis. "Angler Snags Giant World Record Paddlefish at Missouri's Lake of the Ozarks." *Field and Stream.* June 15, 2024.

Harman, Allan. *Psalms.* Mentor Commentaries 2. Ross-shire, GB: Mentor, 2011.

Jamieson, Robert. *Joshua–Esther.* A Commentary, Critical, Experimental, and Practical, on the Old and New Testaments 2. London: William Collins, Sons, n.d.

Jeremias, Joachim. *The Eucharistic Words of Jesus.* New York: Scribner, 1966.

Johnson, Samuel, LL.D. *A Dictionary of the English Language.* Abridged from The Rev. H. J. Todd's Corrected and Enlarged Quarto Edition, by Alexander Chalmers, F.S.A. New York: Barnes & Noble, 1994.

Kauflin, Bob. "Finding the Right Key to Sing In." Worship Matters. May 11, 2009. www.worshipmatters.com/2009/05/11/finding-the-right-key-to-sing-in/.

———. *Worship Matters. Leading Others to Encounter the Greatness of God.* Wheaton, IL: Crossway, 2008.

Kidd, Reggie M. *With One Voice: Discovering Christ's Song in Our Worship.* Grand Rapids: Baker, 2005.

Martin, Ryan J. *Understanding Affections in the Theology of Jonathan Edwards: The High Exercises of Divine Love.* London: T&T Clark, 2019.

Bibliography

McMenamin, Cindi. "What Is the ACTS Prayer Method and How Do You Pray It?" Crosswalk.com. June 17, 2021. https://www.crosswalk.com/faith/prayer/what-is-the-acts-prayer-method-and-how-do-you-pray-it.html/.

Melick, Richard R. *Philippians, Colossians, Philemon*. The New American Commentary 32. Nashville: Broadman & Holman, 199.

Melson, Rick. "Worship: Our Response to His Greatness" Desiring God. April 3, 2016. https://www.desiringgod.org/articles/worship-our-response-to-his-greatness/.

"Men of God: John Calvin's Preface to the Geneva Psalter." *Semper Reformanda*. https:www.seperreformanda.com/men-of-god/john-calvin-index/john-calvins-preface-to-the-genevan-psalter/.

Midwestern Baptist Theological Seminary. Department of Worship Ministries (webpage). https://www.mbts.edu/about/staff/worship-ministries/.

Nemesius of Emesa. "Of the Nature of Man." *Cyril of Jerusalem and Nemesius of Emesa* 4. Edited by William Telfer. The Library of Christian Classics 4. Philadelphia: Westminster, 1955. https://archive.org/details/cyrilofjerusalemooootelf/page/8/mode/2up/.

Newbold, Bradley D. "Worship Strategy for Renewal." Breakout session presented at Resound Summit: Renewed from the Inside Out, Jefferson City, MO, March 2024.

"Of Religious Worship and the Sabbath Day." *The 1689 Baptist Confession of Faith*. Doctrine and Devotion. http://the1689confession.com/1689/chapter-22/.

Pascal, Blaise. *Pascal's Pensées*. New York: E. P. Dutton, 1958. Project Gutenberg, 2006. https://gutenberg.org/files/18269/18269-h/18269-h.htm/.

Payne, Ruby K. *Emotional Poverty in All Demographics: How to Reduce Anger, Anxiety, and Violence in the Classroom*. Highland, TX: aha! Process, 2018.

Polhill, John B. *Acts*. The New American Commentary 26. Nashville: Broadman & Holman, 1992.

Poythress, Vern. "Ezra 3, Union with Christ, and Exclusive Psalmody." *Westminster Journal*. 37 (Fall 1974) 74–94. https://frame-poythress.org/ezra-3-union-with-christ-and-exclusive-psalmody/.

Risbridger, John. *The Message of Worship: Celebrating the Glory of God in the Whole Life*. The Bible Speaks Today. Edited by Derek Tidball. Downers Grove, IL: InterVarsity, 2015.

St. Anselm. *Basic Writings*. Translated by S. N. Deane. La Salle, IL: Open Court, 1962. https://archive.org/details/basicwritings00anse/mode/2up/.

———. *Book of Meditations and Prayers*. Translated by M. Bal. London: Burns & Oates, 1872. https://archive.org/details/StAnselmsBook/page/n45/mode/2up?q=Stir+up+affections.

St. Gregory of Nyssa. *The Soul and Resurrection*. Translated by Catharine P. Roth. Crestwood, New York: St. Vladimir's Seminary, 1993. https://archive.org/details /onsoulresurrectioooogreg/page/n4/mode/1up?q=passion+affection/.

"The Shema," My Jewish Learning. https://www.myjewishlearning.com/article/the-shema/.

Smith, Gary W. *Isaiah 1–39*. The New American Commentary. Edited by E. Ray Clendenen. Nashville: B & H, 2007.

Sproul, R. C. "Strange Fire." *Renew Your Mind*. April 25, 2013. https://www.ligonier.org/learn /articles/strange-fire/.

Spurgeon, Charles H. *The Treasury of David*. London: Marshall Brothers, n.d.

Storms, Sam. *Signs of the Spirit: An Interpretation of Jonathan Edwards' Religious Affections.* Wheaton, IL: Crossway, 2007.

Stosny, Steven. *The Powerful Self: A Workbook of Therapeutic Self-Empowerment.* North Charleston, SC: BookSurge, 2004.

Strong, James. *A Concise Dictionary of the Words in the Greek Testament and The Hebrew Bible.* Bellingham, WA: Logos Research Systems, 2009. Logos Bible Software.

Stuart, Douglas E. *Exodus.* The New American Commentary 2. Nashville: Broadman & Holman, 2006.

"Top-10 Loudest NFL Stadiums Ranked in 2022." Sporty Tell. July 1, 2022. https://sportytell.com/nfl/loudest-nfl-stadiums/.

US Copyright Office. "Subject Matter and Scope of Copyright." https:www.copyright.gov/title17/92chap1.html/.

Vaughan, Curtis. *Acts.* Founders Study Guide Commentary. Cape Coral, FL: Founders, 2009.

Watson, Christopher. "Worship in the Average Church in America." Worship Leader. June 26, 2023. https://worshipleader.com/leadership/worship-in-the-average-church-in-america/.

Yenter, Timothy, and Ezio Vailati. "Samuel Clarke." *Stanford Encyclopedia of Philosophy.* Edited by Edward N. Zalta and Uri Nodelman. Fall 2024. https://plato.stanford.edu/archives/fall2024/entries/clarke/.

www.ingramcontent.com/pod-product-compliance
Lightning Source LLC
Chambersburg PA
CBHW051104160426
43193CB00010B/1304